Improve Your Memory Power

A Simple & Effective Course to Sharpen your Memory in just 30 days!

by

Varinder Aggarwal 'Viren'

Published by:

V&S PUBLISHERS

F-2/16, Ansari road, Daryaganj, New Delhi-110002

☎ 23240026, 23240027 • *Fax:* 011-23240028

info@vspublishers.com • www.vspublishers.com

Online Brandstore: amazon.in/vspublishers

Regional Office : Hyderabad

5-1-707/1, Brij Bhawan (Beside Central Bank of India Lane)

Bank Street, Koti, Hyderabad - 500 095

☎ 040-24737290

vspublishershyd@gmail.com

Follow us on:   

BUY OUR BOOKS FROM: AMAZON FLIPKART

ISBN 978-93-505702-6-5

New Edition

Printed at : Param Offsetters, Okhla, New Delhi–110020

Publisher's Note

We, as V&S publishers are known for Self-Help and Self-Improvement books besides Children Books, Science Encyclopaedia, Storybooks, Dictionaries, Computer, Marketing and Management books and various other books on General Knowledge, Current Affairs, Books for Competitive Examinations, Quiz books, etc., both in English and Hindi comprising about 350 titles. In line with all these books, we are glad to publish yet another masterpiece called ***Improve Your Memory Power*** in the Self-Help and Self-Improvement Category.

The book will immensely benefit all its readers, particularly the school and college students who study and strive hard to excel in their examinations for a bright future ahead! There are various tips for each day in the form of separate chapters in the book that deal exhaustively with the very many ways by which one can develop and improve one's memory, observation, concentration, reasoning and analysing powers. It's basically a *30-day programme* in which the author guarantees a sure development and improvement in one's memory and an overall growth and development of the mind and body.

At the end of each chapter, there's a brief paragraph named *Advice* that guides the readers about how to read the chapter, what are the salient features of the chapter and how will it practically help in improving and sharpening one's memory? At the end of the first page of each chapter, there is a small box containing *Today's Date.* This is a column that has to be filled by the Reader with a Pencil mentioning the date when he/she read the chapter.

The aim is basically to keep a note of the developments and transformations in the reader's mind, behavioural patterns and his entire personality as he proceeds reading one after the other chapters completing all the 30 in 30 days. For this, the chapters have been kept precise and interesting, written in a simple and lucid language. Hope you enjoy reading, learning and improving the faculties of your brain with an outstanding memory!

Contents

Know Your Mind

To begin with the improvement of your memory power, first it is important to know the power of your mind and what all it can do for you. What capacity and strength you already possess and how you can develop it further for much greater achievements. In this chapter, we will discuss the working system of the mind only and not its hardware, that is the brain, or its mechanical setup. It is not of much relevance here.

Human mind is like a rubber-band. The more you use it or the more you stretch it, the sharper and the more capable it becomes to store and analyse greater amounts of information. On the other hand, if you do not use it

Today's Date: __ / __ / ____
(Kindly write with a Pencil)

or let it just idle away, then it becomes highly frustrated, demotivated and useless for ever. And the situation gets worse with the increase in age. Gradually, the thinking, the storing and the analytical abilities subside making the person confused, mentally sick and a liability for all.

The mind has to be trained on a continuous basis to keep it active and in a good working condition so that it keeps delivering the way we want it to. Positive thoughts and new ideas is the ideal food for it. In this way, it remains happy and also keeps the whole functioning of the body at optimum levels.

A positive attitude develops from a strong belief in yourself, your capabilities and your past experiences. Aging of your brain depends directly on your attitude as well as the way of your thinking in day-to-day life. If you remain happy and tension-free for most of your life, then your brain will be more young and healthy even in the older stages of your life. Hence, your mental energies will function like a young adult. It means thinking more clearly, learning and recalling faster, always.

A promise is required from you to yourself today. A dedicated and serious effort from your side is to be applied to the methods suggested in this book. No stress or any kind of worries is required at all. Good results can be obtained only when calmness and patience is observed. Though results will vary from person to person, hence, there should be no competition or copying. You can always improve with another try one after the other, if need be. You will have to put in more efforts with your understanding and as per the improvement of your memory.

Our mind is a genius in its own way. But it is highly underutilised. Not more than ten percent of the mind is used even by the most successful people in the world. Just think if you can increase the working capacity of your mind even by a few percentages only, then it can change your life tremendously. This book will guide you in this direction. Read it, understand it and then apply the techniques as per your own convenience and capacity. Again, I am repeating, please do not compete or copy any other person. Just be yourself, and the world will be yours very soon.

This world has witnessed a great number of intellectuals since time immemorial. There have been great scientists, scholars, mathematicians, artists, saints, spiritual gurus and the like who have harnessed their mind power to such an extent that they could deliver their services, wisdom, inventions and discoveries for the betterment of mankind. Some of them are Newton, Albert Einstein, Graham Bell, John F.Hopkins, Shakuntala Devi, Deepak Chopra and many others. The list is endless.

Exercising and practising on a continuous basis is required to keep the body and the mind fit. As a good and balanced diet with a regular workout is required to keep the body fit, similarly, feeding good, new and positive ideas from time to time are compulsory to keep the mind in optimum health. Physical exercises helps to keep the blood vessels in good condition, lowers cholesterol levels and opens-up blocked arteries as well. This further ensures regular supply of blood and oxygen to the brain. Hence better functioning of the mind.

Human mind is the most complex and the known most capable organ amongst all of the living entities. Mental exercises like playing games, solving puzzles, riddles and mathematical problems are considered good for keeping the mind healthy and active. When the mind is healthy then only it is wise and advisable to undertake any such activity, or schedule a program to enhance the memory power, so that it may not exert any kind of extra pressure on your mind and refrain you from taking due advantage of the memory enhancement program.

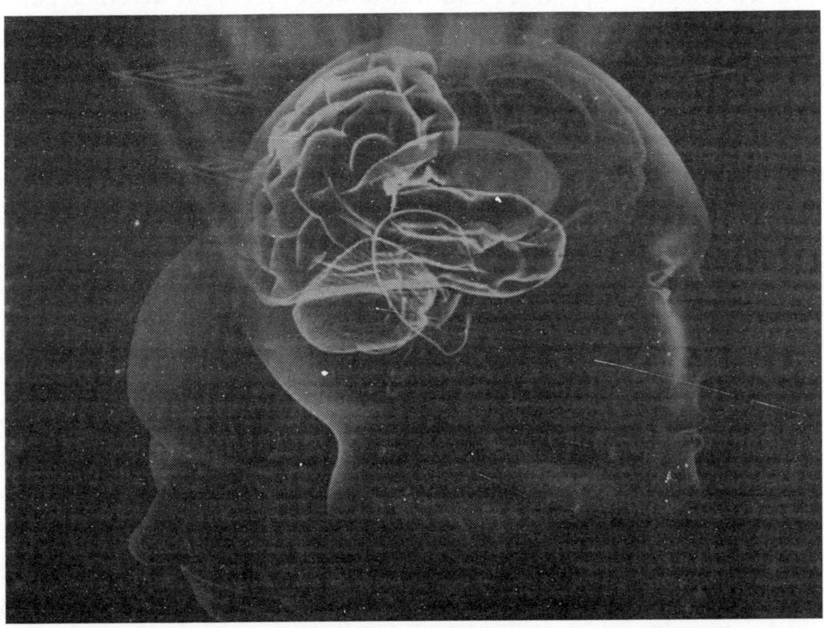

Make a fresh, new beginning in your life from today with great courage and motivation. This attitude will help you erase all your previous bitter experiences and memories. These could have become a potential deterrent in your new learning and during this Memory Enhancement Program.

Now, close your eyes, concentrate and visualise on what you wish to become in future. Do you wish to excel in your studies and be the most brilliant student, or you wish to be the best employee in your company? You may also be willing to be a topper in the Civil Services Examination or looking forward to a rewarding career in sales and marketing. The choices could be many as the choice is yours. This step – visualisation – is very important. Only then the techniques will work for you and give you the desired results.

Memory can be divided into two parts – short-term memory and long-term memory. Short-term memory records each and every thing that it comes across but for a short duration only. It can be momentary like remembering the story and its characters in a movie or a drama.

Long term Memory occurs in two ways. First, on its own, like a fearsome event that flashes across the mind later on and troubles all of us; the beauty and charm of a person which attracted us immensely and sometimes takes us back to that moment; the wonderful taste of a dish which we relished very much that it ticks us every time we come across good delicious food; a picnic spot, a waterfall or some other scenic beauty which had touched our heart, now flashed again while watching television, and so on. Second, when we deliberately repeat and rehearse our syllabus by reading or writing any text, speech, acts or songs, etc.

Functioning of the human mind can be divided into two parts which works simultaneously, the conscious mind and the subconscious mind. The subconscious mind keeps working even when we are asleep whereas the conscious mind somewhat comes to a rest. The subconscious mind controls the thought process of a person, his positive and negative emotions, his happiness and fears, analytical and learning abilities, etc. Hence, it becomes important for us to check every now and then what all is being fed to the mind. Because it itself cannot differentiate between the good and the bad. The subconscious mind will churn out the results only according to the data being supplied to it. And, accordingly it will also be responsible for the mood and emotions of the person.

It is a general known fact that our body or even a mechanical device starts to perform better whenever it is given a break or a rest in its working. The same is applicable to our mind as well. We generally feel refreshed and recharged after a good sound sleep. It happens because we had subjected our body and the conscious mind to rest for a few hours. This kind of sleep is more restful if taken during the night in complete darkness and silence. But as we wake up everything starts working automatically again. This is what we know as the recording and storing by the conscious mind.

Sleeping is a natural phenomenon undertaken by every human being where the body and the conscious mind are subjected to rest. And, that is why they remain in optimum health also. Night is the best time to sleep as our bodies are more attuned to work and rest according to the natural system of sunrise and sunset.

But what about the subconscious mind which has not been given rest for even a moment since our birth? And it is the subconscious mind that directly controls the analysis, the learning and the remembering processes. Proper nourishment, adequate rest and regular exercising are the keys to maintain a good health. Hence, it is our duty to give our subconscious mind good nourishment, necessary rest and exercises to enhance its capacity which in turn will improve your memory.

Nourishment

Nourishment to the mind can be provided in three ways. One, is by eating a balanced diet comprising the required vitamins, minerals, amino acids and other nutrients on a regular basis. Second, is to increase the supply of oxygen in the blood going towards the brain by doing some physical activities like walking or using a bicycle to a nearby grocery store, often using the stairs instead of the lift or by helping your elders in doing some household chores. Third, is to keep meeting positive minded and successful people and discussing with them their success stories, and also by attending other motivational seminars and events.

Rest and Relaxation

Rest and relaxation to the conscious mind is controllable and can be provided in numerous ways like cutting off from one activity and switching over to the other for a few minutes, sleeping or napping, playing, watching TV, switching between subjects, bathing, brisk walking in a nearby park, walking barefoot on moist green grass early morning or stretching exercises, fishing, gardening, etc.

On the other hand, our subconscious mind is uncontrollable and its workings cannot be stopped. But, by practising meditation on a daily basis its working can be slowed down to some extent. And gradually to a greater extent thereby giving our subconscious mind the much needed relaxation and rest, though for a few minutes only. Such kind of rest to the mind multiplies its capacity of working, learning and remembering in due course of time. Besides, there is another big benefit of meditation also. During the initial moments of meditation all the negative emotions, thoughts, experiences and events start getting deleted from the mind automatically. This helps the mind to unclutter itself in the most natural and easiest way. It further helps in greater concentration and hence, in enhanced learning and remembering abilities.

The subconscious mind is more powerful and it influences the conscious mind in daily activities and in important decision making as well. Therefore, with little practice, patience and continuous efforts, we can give directions to our subconscious mind to work according to us and deliver the desired results to us. Our subconscious mind does wonders whenever it is told in a proper way to increase the capacity of the mind towards its workings and learning abilities. And, unknowingly in a few days we are able to work more efficiently and for longer durations with negligible fatigue. So, always feed and direct your mind with good and positive thoughts. The real power and working capacity lie with the subconscious mind, whereas the conscious mind has little role in the learning and remembering activities.

Exercises

What walking does to the body, thinking does to the mind. Both the activities are spontaneous and of utmost importance for our healthy living. Physical and mental exercises, both, help us to keep fit, healthy and in good condition throughout our lives. Physical exercises and activities keep us physically and mentally healthy, and mental exercises and activities also keeps us physically and mentally healthy.

Physical exercises and activities tone up our body physically and in the process regulates the blood circulation which helps to carry more oxygen to the brain. Regulated supply of fresh oxygen to the brain helps to keep the mind calm and relaxed which helps it to work better and faster. Whereas mental exercises and activities keep the mind active and alert which enables it to work better and faster. This in turn helps to keep the body active and healthy because the body is controlled through the mind.

> **Advice:** *Kindly read this chapter at least two to three times today with an interval of four hours minimum. This will prepare your mind and its energies towards the Memory Improvement Programme.*

Prepare Yourself for the Memory Improvement Program

Following are enlisted some of the mental exercises which can prove to be very helpful in keeping the mind active, alert, sharp and focussed besides calm and relaxed as well. These are very simple to learn, adopt, practise and perform in our routine lives.

Indulge Your Mind in Guesswork

These activities will enable the mind to think and act differently in a way which is new to it and it has never done such things before. And gradually, the thinking capacity will start to expand.

- Keeping your eyes closed, roam about in your room and recognise things like the study table, chairs, table lamp, dining table, centre table, flower pot, curtains, cupboard, TV, computer, music system, etc., with your hands only.
- Place some local currency coins in a box and try to recognise and differentiate them.
- Safely stand on a roadside and try to distinguish between the different vehicles passing by on the basis of their engine sounds and horns.
- Whenever in a park try to recognise various flowers as per their fragrances.
- Try to guess and cross check the change in temperatures at home and other places that you happen to visit.
- Try to bathe with your eyes closed. Follow and perform all the routine activities with your guesswork.
- With your eyes closed try to recognise what all has been served to you during your meals through its odour or as felt by your hands.

Today's Date: __ / __ / ____
(Kindly write with a Pencil)

Try Using 'The Other Hand'

(**Note:** If you perform most of your routine jobs with your right hand then try using your left hand as the main hand. And if you are using your left hand for undertaking most of your routine jobs then use your right hand as the main hand in the following exercises).

Most of the people use their right hand for doing their routine jobs in this world. It means their left brain is being used more and the right side of the brain remains idle for most of the time. Gradually, when we start trying to use our other hand, that would be the left hand here, then we are giving ourselves a chance to kick start in using our right side of the brain also. Using both of our hands will also save a lot of our precious time as well besides enhancing of our memory power. In this way, with the following activities we can increase the working and storing capacity of our mind.

- Try to play and get hold of the ludo dice, table tennis racquet, badminton racquet, carrom board striker, chess, etc., with the other hand.
- Try eating your meals with a spoon or writing, drawing or painting with a brush, playing a musical instrument, etc.,. with your other hand.
- Try to switch on your television, computer, laptop, air-conditioner, music system, etc., and also using their remote control devices with your other hand.
- Try combing your hair, shaving, brushing your teeth, brushing your shoes, dialling a number on the phone or mobile handset, etc., with your other hand.
- Try cutting, peeling or eating fruits and vegetables, preparing and cooking your food, washing utensils, gardening and watering the plants, cleaning and greasing your vehicle, etc., with your other hand.
- Also, try to change sides and directions. Like, change your side while getting onto your bicycle or other two-wheeler vehicle. This should be tried before the vehicle has started moving. Also try to kick-start it using the other foot.

Advice: *Kindly read this chapter at least two to three times today with an interval of four hours minimum, and practise the activities that have been suggested to you. It will not be easy but it could turn out to be interesting.*

***

DAY 3

Observation, Reasoning and Analysis

The following activities will help you to mould your thinking process by carrying out such actions that are different from the normal way of your life. Such activities are termed as co-curricular activities and are also associated with our studies in some way or the other.

- Solve different kinds of puzzles. It could be mathematical calculations, crosswords or re-arrangement of words in English or any other language, general knowledge questions, etc.
- Participate in group plays, acting, song and dance competitions, debates and lectures, etc.
- Participate in science exhibitions and competitions, seminars, fairs, matches, fetes, games and sports held in your school or educational institution.
- Start a new hobby, like drawing or painting, sketching, writing articles or poems, stamps or coins collection or even learning a new language, etc.
- Observing plants or flowers, insects, birds or animals, and gathering information about their formation and existence.
- Reverse counting is also an interesting activity, like 10,9,8, … 1,0.
- In the beginning, see and count in reverse and after some time repeat the reverse counting verbally without seeing it written anywhere. Now gradually increase the counts, i.e. starting from 10 to reverse, then 20 to reverse and then 30 to reverse and so on.
- Imitate an actor, a celebrity or a famous personality for his acting skills, his other style or any other thing you like about him.
- Experimenting and playing games and sports in a

Today's Date: __ / __ / ____
(Kindly write with a Pencil)

different way or apply some new idea in using playing equipments like the balls, racquets, shuttle cock, dice, playing cards, etc. Try to throw up and rotate two or more balls by your hands.

- Try dribbling the basket ball or any other ball in a new way with both your hands at the ground as well as in the air or with a bat or a racquet.

General Precautions

- All activities should be undertaken with great care. Neither hurt yourself nor it should become a nuisance for others or look much absurd while practising.
- In the beginning some of the activities could appear to be boring or awkward or you may even fail in the early attempts as well, but these are going to enhance your memory to a great extent. So, patiently follow and practise them. Ultimately you are going to enjoy the benefits.
- These activities not only open up new avenues of thinking but also help to entertain, relax and refresh your mind as well.
- Undertake these activities in a rather joyful and playful mood. In this way it will become quite easy to grasp and practice with the new type of activities. It will not exert any extra pressure on the mind.
- And finally, the more you practice the better it will get with each passing day and gradually expand the capacity of your mind.

As you already know we humans seldom use even ten percent of our mind. Now think that when ten percent can do marvellous wonders in the world in inventions and discoveries in various fields like science and technology, space, medicine, computers, automobiles, telecom, etc., then think what can an enhanced capability of the mind can do towards the personal development of a person as well as towards the increased happiness of mankind.

Advice: Practise all the activities at least three to four times today. Never mind about your performance or the failed attempts. It will get better with every next attempt.

Develop Good Learning

Learning is a continuous process which happens in multiple ways. It starts with your very first breath since the birth itself. It is a natural phenomenon that your mind understands, learns and remembers logical facts more easily, and all those things that it comes across repeatedly. Hence, practising something regularly and repeatedly is surely bound to deliver better results. For this, observation power should also be good.

Natural Ways of Learning

Learning takes place through seeing and observing, touching, feeling and sensing, hearing, smelling, tasting and recognising. Whatever stage of sensing your body passes through is recorded in the mind immediately. And gradually, a database gets created of all that has been seen, heard or felt. This is a natural process of learning which will continue throughout your lives till the last breath.

Today's Date: __ / __ / ____
(Kindly write with a Pencil)

Formal Education

The other learning process begins with your formal education in the school, through normal teachings, coachings and other training programs undertaken during the school life or during professional upgradations. Whatever you read, hear, study or observe is recorded in the mind. Whenever you practise your course material time and again, it becomes ingrained in your mind with repeated learnings. But for proper understanding, good learning and recalling abilities, you need to have a good and sharp memory power.

Learning by Analysis

This kind of learning takes place when we get answers and solutions to our difficulties and problems. It is again a natural phenomenon that whenever we are confronted with a problem, we approach our mind and our mind starts to work out probable solutions at the subconscious level. The mind approaches and analyses the database and previous experiences. This process sometimes is able to give suitable solutions within a few seconds or may even extend to a number of days. Guessing is also an integral part of this process.

Here are a few examples

1. Many times, we try to guess and ascertain the timings during the day, be it early morning, the noon or the evening, whenever we are stranded without a watch or a clock nearby.
2. Sometimes, when all of a sudden, we have to visit an ailing relative in another city at odd hours, choosing the right mode of transport, be it public or private, becomes a matter of concern. We also have to consider about the safety and convenience of the people travelling with us, the approximate timing of reaching there, carrying a doctor along or any other relevant help, etc.
3. Analysis plays a major role in choosing the right life partner for marriage or even a business partner as well. We have to analyse and finalise as per our criteria and suitability from all the given facts and conditions mentioned.

It has been felt by many people that the mind works better and faster when it is in a relaxed state of mind. It generally gives incorrect ideas and answers when it is in tension or extreme pressure. So always try to remain calm and peaceful and also try to see the positive side of the situation. This will in turn help your mind to give you favourable solutions.

Learning by Hit and Trial Method

This is another common method of learning. Here learning takes place when you will continuously keep on solving a problem. Repeatedly keep on trying new ideas and techniques in old and new ways to be able to solve the problem. And soon you will start feeling comfortable in the given situation. The more you practise the better it will get. Moreover, you will also learn how to practise better with the next attempt.

A few examples are:

1. A very common situation arises while unlocking a door in the initial days when we are unable to find the right key for it in a bunch. The situation worsens when we are in a hurry. But, later on, with regular usage we are able to recognise the right keys for particular doors rather easily.
2. Similar situation arises with a light and switch board. In the initial days, it is hard to remember which switch is connected to which particular light, bulb or fan. But gradually, we are able to recognise the right switch button with more comfort and ease.
3. The same technique also comes into use when we are solving games and puzzles. It happens more with crosswords or while playing scrabble where various combination of words have to be formed and worked out.

There are various factors that influence the learning process in any person. The same is applicable to keep the information intact, accurate and for faster recalling. Hence, these methods are important afterwards also. They are as follows:

Willingness, Cheerful Mood and Positive Attitude

Learning is faster and more accurate when there is willingness, cheerful mood and positive attitude to practise or observe something. This is a natural phenomenon. Positive affirmations also help to keep intact and further develop positive attitude towards life in general.

Satisfaction Level

All those activities, assignments and subjects which are read and understood easily by the mind have a greater satisfaction level. And whenever and wherever the satisfaction level is good, the learning also tends to be good.

Inspiration

Inspiration comes from within and works wonders towards the learning process. A person gets inspired by the success and achievements of others. Then he also develops similar interests and feelings to focus and concentrate better and work harder towards his studies or work.

Motivation

A person feels motivated in undertaking an activity when he begins to visualise that he is an important part of the success story. Here the motivation takes place when a person thinks about his own achievements, whereas when he hears about other people's success, he feels inspired to work towards his goals.

Practice and Repetition

Practising and repeating the course material by reading and writing results into more accurate and faster learning. It also eliminates any chances of mistakes with regard to tenses, spellings, punctuation or grammar, etc. Pronunciation and communication of a language gets better with regular listening, reading aloud and conversing with other people.

Face Challenges Boldly

Whenever we start something new or afresh, we all come across certain types of problems, obstructions and challenges. It could be with regard to accepting and adopting the new activities and changes that starts taking place in our daily routine life. It may also demand a change in our lifestyle and thinking. These challenges could be laziness, un-readiness to adopt new ways of thinking, changes in living style or diet patterns, etc. It could also be certain type of fears or phobia or may arise on account of shortage of time and funds. But, remember that there are always ways and means to fulfil your desires. You only have to look, plan and work differently now to participate in new activities and get used to it.

Remain Active and Alert

Whenever we are active and alert in our approach, we tend to come across several new activities and events taking place around us. Such an approach also leads us to opportunities where we can develop our talents further and learn newer things. Despite our great learning, knowledge, achievements and success, there still remains millions of things which we are not even aware of. So, always be open to fresh and new ideas with an attitude to learn something new on a continuous basis.

> **Advice:** Kindly read this chapter at least two to three times today with an interval of four hours minimum. This will prepare your mind and its energies towards the Memory Improvement Programme.

Develop Your Observation Power Part – I

DAY 5

Good Observation leads to Good Analysis which further leads to Good Learning. Good observation can be initiated and developed quite easily. Noticing things and events more carefully and minutely results into good observation.

Let us take a look at a simple example:

A	HONESTYIS THE BEST POLICY	B	HONESTY IS THE IS BEST POLICY
C	HONESTY IS THE THE BEST POLICY	D	ONESTY IS THE BEST POLECY

Of the four boxes A, B, C, D shown above, only one box contains the correct phrase and the rest others are incorrect in some way or the other. Which one is the correct one and what are the mistakes in the other sentences? Kindly find it out for yourself and get it checked by your parents, teachers or any other elder person.

People having good observation are found to commit fewer mistakes as compared to other people. Good observation leads to good intellect which develops a cautious approach in a person forever. Such people tend to learn from their bad experiences as well as from the bad consequences faced for the mistakes and carelessness committed by other people.

Psychologists are also of the opinion that people having good observation power also have better intellect and good memory. Such people tend to learn things more

Today's Date: __ / __ / ____
(Kindly write with a Pencil)

quickly and are also able to retain it for longer durations and with greater accuracy. So, it becomes important for people to improve their observation power first. It is especially important for those who are slow or careless in observing even the simple things or events taking place around them.

Before taking up the exercises for improving your observation power, let us first prepare ourselves in the following ways:

- Start reading good detective stories and novels. Also start watching detective serials and movies. Detective works are based on observing minutest details of the place of crime, activities and emotions of the people related with the event, etc. This will not only help you but train you greatly in your observing and remembering process. This will also make you more cautious in your approach required in general day-to-day living.
- Start collecting information about the inventions and discoveries taking place around the world. A lot of hard work, dedication, patience, caution and minute observation are required to carry out all such activities. Try to find out and learn what were the techniques engaged and various methods adopted by the team involved. This will help you to develop your observation power to a great extent. Make a separate folder for each invention and discovery.
- In your school, office or place of work, try to get involved in activities or be a part of projects which require some kind of research or investigations necessary to accomplish the assignment. This will teach and train you about the techniques required to carry out the study.

Advice: *Enquire from your friends or colleagues or from the nearby bookshop about the detective stories, books or novels available with them. Try to borrow such books on returnable basis only, at least in the beginning. Similarly, make enquiries about the TV series or movies based on detective stories. The choice is yours.*

The idea here is to learn observation, and how these detectives observe and take into account the minutest of details in their investigations without missing out to note anything.

Develop Your Observation Power
Part – II

Here are some exercises to improve your observation power. You may maintain a diary for this purpose as well.

(To be carried out before you go to sleep at night, for at least one month.)

(Answers once written, should not be erased, altered or cancelled).

(With daily practice, accuracy will start happening on its own).

At what time you woke up in the morning? = ...

At what time you had your bath? = ...

At what time you had your breakfast? = ...

What all you had in your breakfast? = ...

What dress you wore today? = ...

What was the colour of your dress? = ...

Were you feeling comfortable in it? = Yes / No / Okay

Did you feel more confident today? = ...

Or did you feel lazy and tiresome today? = ...

How others judged you today? = Good / Better / Normal

What you liked about yourself today? = ...

What you disliked about yourself today? = ...

> **Advice:** Maintain a daily record for at least six to eight months. This will greatly enhance your observation. Gradually, you will also come to know about what others are thinking about you.

***

Today's Date: __ / __ / ____
(Kindly write with a Pencil)

Practice Session - I

I hope you must have thoroughly read all the chapters till now. I also think that you must have followed the advice mentioned at the end of every chapter. I hope you must have started working on the methods suggested and must be enjoying them as well.

Today we will practise some of the exercises again (the exercises we have already practised. However, repeat these exercises to improve your memory further. Please don't ignore these exercises before we proceed further.) This is being done to assess your understanding, learning and development in this regard.

Indulge Your Mind in Some Guesswork

These activities will enable the mind to think and act differently in a new way as it may not do such things before. And gradually, the thinking capacity will begin to expand.

- Keeping your eyes closed, roam about in your room and recognise things like the study table, chairs, table lamp, dining table, centre table, flower pot, curtains, cupboard, TV, computer, music system, etc., with your hands only.
- Place some local currency coins in a box and try to recognise and differentiate them.
- Try to bathe with your eyes closed. Follow and perform all the routine activities with your guesswork.
- With your eyes closed, try to recognise what all has been served to you during your meals through its odour or as felt by your hands.

Try Using 'The Other Hand'

(**Note:** If you perform most of your routine jobs with your right hand, then try using your left hand as the main hand. And if you are using your left hand for undertaking most of your

Today's Date: __ / __ / ____
(Kindly write with a Pencil)

routine jobs, then use your right hand as the main hand in the following exercises).

- Try to play and get hold of the ludo dice, table tennis racquet, badminton racquet, carrom board striker, chess, etc. with the other hand.
- Try eating your meals with a spoon or writing, drawing or painting with a brush, playing a musical instrument, etc. with your other hand.
- Try to switch on your television, computer, laptop, air conditioner, music system, etc. and also using their remote control devices with your other hand.
- Try combing your hair, shaving, brushing your teeth, polishing your shoes, dialling a number on the phone or mobile handset, etc. with your other hand.
- Try cutting, peeling or eating fruits and vegetables, preparing for and cooking your food, washing utensils, gardening and watering the plants, cleaning and greasing your vehicle, etc. with your other hand.
- Also, try to change sides and directions. Like, change your side while getting on to your bicycle or other two-wheeler vehicle. This should be tried before the vehicle has started moving. Also try to kick-start it using the other foot.

Mould Your Thinking

The following activities will help you to mould your thinking process by carrying out such actions that are different from the normal way of your life. Such activities are termed as co-curricular activities and are also associated with our studies in some way or the other.

- Solve different kinds of puzzles. It could be mathematical calculations, crosswords or rearrangement of words in English or any other language of your choice, general knowledge questions, etc.
- Start a new hobby, like drawing or painting, sketching, writing articles or poems, stamps or coins collection or even learning a new language, etc.
- Observing plants or flowers, insects, birds or animals, and gathering information about their formation and existence.
- Reverse counting is also an interesting activity, like 10,9,8, … 1,0.

- In the beginning, see and count in reverse, and after some time repeat the reverse counting verbally without seeing it written anywhere. Now gradually increase the counts, i.e., starting from 10 to reverse, then 20 to reverse and then 30 to reverse and so on.
- Imitate an actor, a celebrity or a famous personality for his acting skills, his other style or any other thing you like about him.
- Try dribbling the basket ball or any other ball in a new way with both your hands at the ground as well as in the air or with a bat or a racquet.

> **Advice:** *Put a tick mark with a pencil in front of the activity you enjoyed doing it. You may also put a cross mark or mention a remark in front of the activity you could not perform correctly.*

DAY 8

Develop Your Observation Power Part – III

Take up any one of the following activities today to be a part of the improving your learning, remembering and recalling process. Rest of the activities should be taken later on to improve upon your observation power.

- Begin this with your own room first. Facing an empty wall, start writing down all the things, big or small, present in the room without looking back at them. When finished, now check it with all the things present in the room.
- Repeat the same exercise when you visit some public office, exhibition, museums, fairs, fetes, hotels and restaurants, etc. You may also note down their decorations at the entrance, on the floors, walls, roof or on the pillars, etc., and your opinions about it. Gradually, you will come to know the differences in the thinking of people from the various places visited.
- Repeat the same exercise when you visit your friend or someone in the neighbourhood. Upon return, note down all that you have noticed in their house, room, lobby or terrace. The idea is only to gauge the speed and accuracy of your observation. Now check your list when you visit them the next time. Judge your accuracy yourself. Now, you may either destroy or tear down the noting or simply hand

Today's Date: __ / __ / ____
(Kindly write with a Pencil)

it over to the respective house owner stating your good intentions in doing so.

- Similarly, whenever you happen to visit some other city, town, a village, countryside or even some other country, observe the people of that country. Also pay attention to their customs and rituals, language, currency, their way of living, etc. Such exercises will increase your observation power, your learning about new things as well as increase your memory power.

Advice: *This is all for today. It may seem to be simple and small at the beginning, but it is time consuming. It will require a good deal of your energy and concentration as well. Hence, get started.*

DAY 9

Develop Your Observation Power Part – IV

Below are mentioned some common activities to gauge your observation power. Taking up the following activities will make you more concerned even about the small things taking place around you.

- How many steps are there in the stairs of your building, your school, your college or your place of work and how these stairs are further sub-divided?
- You may also begin noticing and counting the stairs wherever you go. This will help you great extent in enhancing your observation and remembering skills.
- Prepare a record as to how much time was spent in various routine activities during the day, like waking up and leaving for school or office, time spent during travelling, in recreational activities, in relaxing or watching TV or spending time with friends, etc.
- Maintain a record of your income and earnings from other sources. Also prepare a chart of necessary and entertainment expenses.
- What is the normal time taken to reach the nearest bus stop, park or supermarket if you go walking, by your bicycle or by your car?
- How much time do you generally take to get ready when you are going to your school or office, to play, to the market or when going to attend

Today's Date: __ / __ / ____
(Kindly write with a Pencil)

some party or a function?

- Similarly, how much time do other members in the family take for all the activities stated above.
- With your eyes closed, try touching specific objects in your room, your house, certain plants and flowers in a garden, etc. If necessary, take someone's help to judge as well as protect you from getting hurt.
- Generally, what is your heart-beat or pulse rate when you have just woken up, back from school or office, after outdoor sports or exercising, after cooking or gardening, before and after meals, after prayers or meditation, etc.?

Advice: All these activities could seem to be somewhat awkward and absurd in the beginning, and noting down even more boring and wastage of time. But it will help you immensely in the long run.

Gradually, you will start noticing and recording the time consumed in various activities at the subconscious level. This in turn will help you in planning and managing your time more efficiently.

DAY 10

Develop your Imagination Part - I

Imagination is an activity of the mind of thinking about something which is non-existent. And it could also be about thinking something in a different format from its current shape or usage. Good imagination is the result of a well-nourished and a fertile subconscious mind. Good imagination has led to innumerable inventions, discoveries and other creative works throughout the world since time immemorial. Good imagination activates an astounding kind of courage and great mental strength within oneself.

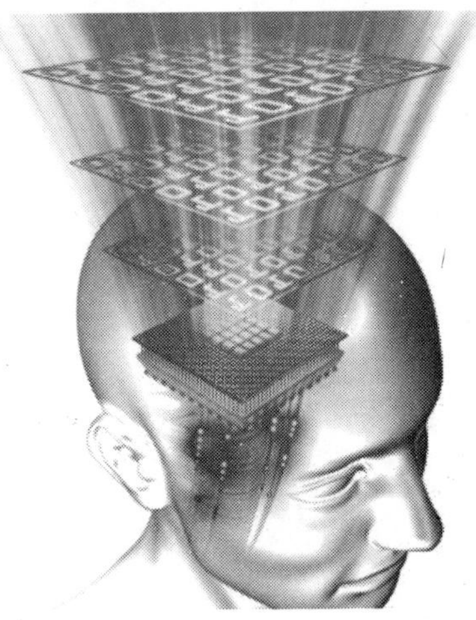

Good observation acts as a raw material for good imagination which helps a person to achieve and deliver great services beneficial for the mankind. Here meditation gives the subconscious mind the required fertilizers to process the desired results whenever an enquiry or requirement is fed to the mind.

All those people who possess or have developed their observation power and further strengthened their imagination are often able to deliver new kind of products and services. It could either be related to a new breakthrough in medicines, information technology, biotech, telecommunications, engineering, sports or even general goods and services.

All the people possessing good memory power are able to harness their mental energies

Today's Date: __ / __ / ____
(Kindly write with a Pencil)

effectively. They are also able to visualise their goals and plan out their working techniques in advance. This keeps them motivated enough which enables them to work continuously for hours and days altogether. They do not withdraw till they are able to make substantial improvements and achievements in their specific area of research. Without imagination and creative insights, it would be difficult to conceive new ideas as well as progress towards one's goals.

It is the power of good imagination and deep visualisation that many people are able to achieve their desired targets and positions in life. These positions can be in the field of education, sports or even in the office they work. The path towards success gets laid on its own. Only it has to be followed with honesty and devotion. Such methods have also led to personality development as well as happiness in relationships.

Visualisation of your goals is also one of the types of imagination of the results you wish to achieve. It greatly helps to keep the tedious process of hard work interesting and rather easy than being boring and cumbersome. The person also remains motivated. For a sportsman, for example, visualisation of achieving the No.1 position always plays a very important role towards his success besides all the hard work, practising and persistence that he has devoted to his game.

Visualisation of success works at the subconscious level giving a person an extra push, courage and extra strength of mind from within. It helps to break the normal thought process and enables him to emerge as a winner. That is why we often hear about new records being created either in the field of sports, higher percentages and rankings being touched in studies or a breakthrough achieved in some new research.

Imagination and visualisation of success have a small negative side also. But it is only for those who begin living in the world of day-dreaming, thus neglecting the basic facts and hard truths of the actual world. Many times people get lost in the yet-to-be-achieved success and its recognition thereof. They also start discriminating themselves as being superiors from the others. This greatly hampers their preparations for the development of their positive attitude. It also has a devastating bearing on their life if they happen to miss out or fail to achieve their desired targets. But, we must not forget that the technique of 'visualisation of success' works better when there are no rules, regulations or boundaries. Hence, due care should be taken in this respect.

Imagination is a natural system of your thought process. It is a continuous process wherein you may think or visualise anything randomly. Whenever good things or good ideas flash through your mind, you may start feeling good, happy or positive. But whenever your mind comes across some bad or negative thoughts or emotions, you may start feeling lonely, fearsome and demotivated towards life. Your good previous thoughts, experiences and happy moments lay the foundation for good imagination, and vice versa. Good imagination also leads to good planning. It is a psychological process which takes place on its own.

Imagination, many a times, can look to be absurd or meaningless. It is just a thinking or a weird guess. It has nothing to do with the actual logical world. But it is not the reality. Imagination can differ from person to person because each person has their own unique way of thinking. One person's experiences of life, observation, analysis and remembrance at the conscious and the subconscious level will also be different.

Our needs and desires also inspire the subconscious mind to think out of the box, i.e. to think or imagine differently. You must have certainly heard the famous saying: "Necessity is the Mother of Invention". Yes, this is very much true. Our necessities also give us a push to accomplish things in a different way every now and then. It is more prevalent in our daily routine lives as well. It is the inherent nature of human beings to lessen their burden of work and the time consumed in any process. Hence, the mind is continuously searching for new ways to simplify our workings. And the actual force gets developed from within, that is through our own imagination.

People with creative abilities are often found to either draw, paint, write or make different things to express their imaginations. And in the process, an idea might acquire the shape of a reality or an important invention. Like, for example, some person might have initially drawn the image of a man flying with his wings like a bird. Later on, Wright brothers went on develop a flying machine on similar pattern and thinking, though after a lot of hard work and trials. This ultimately resulted into one of the most important inventions in the history of mankind. There are many more examples in this regard.

The automotive world in which we live in today and cannot do without has developed out of the need to simplify our day-to-day workings. Machines have decreased our physical labour substantially as well as made our lives more comfortable. It has also saved a lot of our hard pressed and precious time.

A few common examples are washing machines for clothes and dish washer for utensils; ceiling or table fan to give us the feeling of a breeze; an air conditioner which changes the temperature of the room or a building to protect us from heat; a heater to protect us from cold; a juicer which squeezes juice out of fruits faster for us to consume; a grinder which crushes various eatables to smaller units in only a few seconds; a grinder in a flour mill which turns wheat into flour which is further baked into making bread and other eatables, etc. Now you can yourself analyse the world around you and judge for yourself the importance of good imagination.

Similarly, the following examples also might have been the result of someone's imagination or creativity –

- A car, bus, train, boat, ship or an aeroplane carrying many people in a single journey
- A double-decker bus, train or an aeroplane with more seating capacity
- A rocket carrying people to space
- A metro train plying along with other traffic in the city
- Working in shifts in an office or a factory as per one's convenience with the help of time punching machines
- A zoo where we can safely see many of the big and other dangerous animals found in the forest
- A match stick, a stove lighter, a candle, etc. used in the kitchen
- A pencil, an eraser, a sharpener, an ink pen or a ball pen, etc., are different easy-to-use tools for writing
- A blackboard or a chalk used in a school
- A television or radio to entertain us
- A refrigerator to keep and preserve eatables at a colder temperature
- Live telecast of a program or a sports match being played miles away on radio, television or the internet

- Blending of Ethanol, a sugarcane by-product, and mixing it with petrol; and research work on other renewable energy sources and so on…

Advice: *Read this chapter at least three to four times during the day. The more the better. This will leave a deep mark on your mind with respect to the workings of imagination. This will also help you to gain an upper hand and self-confidence during this memory improvement program.*

Develop your Imagination Part – II

Though developing your imagination power is somewhat a tricky matter, the following examples will help you to look, think and analyse the world around you in a different way. These may look awkward, funny or absolute foolishness at first, but as I said earlier also, it is just another way of thinking or merely a weird guess. Who knows, some of you might create something useful, interesting or entertaining out of it someday.

- For Men – Think about a man around you who is a thorough gentleman who dresses well, has good habits and takes care of his family and responsibilities well. Now, imagine that you are gradually adopting his good habits and are now feeling more confident.
- For Women – Similarly, think about a woman who is perfect in your opinion. Who takes care of her family well and manages the upkeep of her house as well as herself very well. Now, imagine that you are also beautiful, possess good dressing sense and are being looked upon by others more respectfully.
- On a day when you are feeling extremely tired, worried or de-motivated, think about your favourite movie or sports star, a scientist or a successful businessman. Now, imagine yourself to be similarly confident, happy and contented. Soon, you will be surprised to feel a sudden gush of strength inside you surrounded by positive energy all around.
- Imagine and create a new tune on a musical instrument for an existing favourite song or for a nursery rhyme you had liked.
- Try to develop a new recipe or prepare a commonly known dish in a new way by your imagination. You may also imagine to recall the taste

Today's Date: __ / __ / ____
(Kindly write with a Pencil)

about some dishes you had appreciated in the past.

- Imagine about automobiles that use air pressure, salty ocean water or other liquid – partly or solely to operate.
- A car which may ply on the road, fly in the air as well as swim in water.
- Imagine about a new spaceship that would ferry more passengers in lesser time to the moon.
- Imagine to clear the snow on roads with the heat of your vehicle's engine.
- Think of developing new kind of life jackets which are bigger and much lighter to save larger number of people during floods.
- Think of developing other additional uses of the mobile phones, television remote control devices or their batteries, etc.
- Think about new methods of recycling of used, torn or worn out clothes, shoes, items made of paper or wood, etc.
- Also, think of using minimal energy sources and creating lesser wastage in the process. And so on…

Sometimes you will have to work in a silly way also to create something different out of your imagination. Just start doing and your mind will guide you further.

> **Caution:** *You shoulod not think of doing something that goes against nature or harm plants and animals in any way. It should also not be against the law of the land or the society. That would be the negative side of your imagination.*

Improve Your Decision-Making Power

Decisions are the commands that are passed on to the mind to initiate action in order to fulfil the desired objectives. Decisions are an integral part of our lives. Our mind takes scores of decisions every now and then to think, act or move forward.

Some of the decisions are prompt that are taken in our daily routine life which begins from the very moment we wake up. These could be the choice of dress to be worn on that day, a specific breakfast, the mode of transport, calling certain friends or clients while travelling, drinking tea, coffee or a cold drink to keep oneself refreshed and so on. There are endless decisions we take that we even do not notice but they are somehow, automatically initiated by the mind and acted upon.

There are some decisions that are taken for short term, medium term and long term as well. Short term decisions could be regarding a crash course helpful along with the current studies, choosing a holiday destination for the upcoming vacations, making arrangements for birthday, anniversary or bachelor party next month and so on.

Medium-term decisions could be regarding taking up a hobby course, changing a job, taking up a

Today's Date: __ / __ / ____
(Kindly write with a Pencil)

new assignment or enrolling for a management program along with the existing job for upgradation, renovation or extention to your house and so on.

Long-term decisions are those which will affect you throughout your life. Such decisions could be choosing the stream of studies you wish to pursue like engineering, medicine, business studies or humanities. It could also be while choosing an interest for your livelihood like singing, acting, writing or even contesting elections to serve the people of your country, migrating to some other state or country permanently or with regard to choosing the right life partner for your marriage, etc.

Decision making is not an easy process for everyone. Many a times, people come across several doubts, such as if(s) and but(s) that it confuses them completely and renders them hopeless and clueless as what decision would be the most suitable for them. A few examples are:

- What *if* I did not feel comfortable in wearing cotton clothes today?
- It would have been better *if* I could take my car to the office today.
- Though I am preparing for the exams myself *but* coaching would also have been beneficial.
- I would have felt better *if* I had taken some tomato soup instead of a cup of coffee just before lunch time.
- I could have slept better *if* I had taken a bath before sleeping *but* could have caught cold as well.
- It would have been better *if* I had also studied law after graduation.
- How would I survive in another country *if* I could not get a suitable job or work? And so on...

All those people who have developed and trained their minds since their early childhood are more apt in solving such issues quite easily. It further paves the way for their success because they do not get stuck up easily like others. They courageously move forward towards accomplishing their goals. Doubts demotivate people very badly and have devastating effects on their lives. Previous experiences and sharpness of their minds help people in overcoming their doubts and they are able to move forward in life confidently.

Self-confidence is a positive step in this direction. People holding high positions and in-charge of other authoritative designations are found to have greater amount of self-confidence as well as higher intellectual powers because decisions taken by such people will affect a large number of people of their company, their society or their nation as a whole. Hence, intellectual powers should be improved and enhanced so that you can take your decisions more speedily and accurately. A decision once taken should be implemented immediately without much delay or doubt. Otherwise, the objective of the decision would fail to deliver the desired results.

Methods to improve your decision-making abilities:

- Start maintaining a small notepad or a pocket diary with the current year dates with yourself always.
- Now, as per the dates printed on the diary, after thinking carefully, start noting down the works and pending assignments as per the availability of your time and convenience.
- A work once mentioned on a certain date should be undertaken on that date itself without any kind of delay due to laziness or mood swings.
- Before taking any decision, you must ensure your objective very well. Then only the work will begin and be implemented properly.
- Always seek and hire the advice and services of a professional like an advocate, a chartered accountant or a doctor wherever required.
- Besides the above professional help, you must also equip yourself with the information from other sources for your own knowledge. It will help you in taking decisions more effectively.
- Refer your previous decisions and experiences thereof in taking decisions. It is quite possible that you are confronted with similar types of problems in your field of weaknesses and shortcomings.
- Also, try to analyse and solve problems with a different perspective. Such an approach also works wonders.
- First, calmly try to understand the problem in its actual sense that is troubling you, then only work on finding its solution.
- A written down approach is a better way than analysing and solving problems verbally. Make a separate list for everything. Like for things available and for things that are short, etc. It will

avoid any kind of unnecessary burden on your mind.

Precautions

- Never take decisions in haste.
- Relaxation also proves a boon while taking decisions. Sometimes postponing a decision for some time is quite helpful.
- Never take decisions due to shortage of time.
- Never take decisions when you are being pressurised by others.
- Never take decisions without analysing each and every aspect of the concerned subject matter.
- Never take decisions in a state of intoxication.
- Never take decisions while you are feeling tired, worried or feeling drowsy.
- Never take decisions when you are very busy in some other work or while talking with somebody.

Your decisions should not only be fruitful to you, but also be acceptable by the society you are living in. Your decisions should never work against the interests of the common man. Otherwise, the negative effects of the same will certainly affect you and your family any time in future. Hence, take due considerations with enough time and intelligence while taking decisions.

> **Advice:** Read this chapter at least three to four times during the day, today.

DAY 13

Improve Your Concentration Part – I

'Concentration' means to devote all your energy and efforts in getting a certain work completed without any kind of distractions or disturbances. It enables faster learning in lesser time with good understanding of the subject matter. Along with firm determination, it further helps our minds to work better towards storing and recalling information at a later date.

Human mind is the most powerful organ amongst all the other forms of living entities in this world. It has great power and capabilities hidden inside it. Our mind undertakes multiple tasks every second. Its power is immeasurable. Hence, when the mind is focussed on a single task, it is able to deliver astonishing results. All great scholars, scientists and other successful people undertake their tasks with full zeal, determination and most importantly, concentration.

Today's Date: __ / __ / ____
(Kindly write with a Pencil)

Methods to Improve Your Concentration and Focus

- Wherever you are sitting or standing alone or in a queue, close your eyes, take a deep breath slowly and release it slowly. Repeat this 5-10 times. This will always help to calm you down and help focusing your mind.
- You may undertake this activity several times during the day. This will ensure a small rest to your mind and further help it to work better.
- Undertake only one activity at a time whenever possible. Accomplish your tasks one by one.
- Do not let your mind wander away from the task at hand. Finish it first, then only you may look at other things.
- Always use a stable table and chair while studying. This greatly helps to improve your concentration and avoid any kind of disturbances.
- Always use good quality stationery. In this way, the distractions are minimal and hence, you can focus better on your work.
- Developing good understanding and interest in the subject matter also helps in improving concentration, and vice versa.
- Devise your own ways of creating interest in studies or works that seem to be boring or of lesser interest to you. Take the help and guidance of seniors and other successful people in that particular field.
- Always wear neat and clean clothes to feel comfortable and hence, focus better on your work.
- Always take lighter meals preferably 4-5 times during the day instead of 2 or 3 heavy meals. This not only ensures optimum health but also results into better concentration.
- Try to avoid too much oily, spicy, cold or fast food. These foods also make you lethargic and unhealthy which results into a lot of distractions.
- Prefer home-cooked food most of the time. And eat food when it is being served hot. It enables good digestion, good health and good concentration.
- Regular bathing also refreshes and energises the body and mind together. It greatly relaxes and calms the mind and helps to

concentrate better.

- Use natural light for most of the time. Using artificial light for long durations stresses the mind more and disturbs concentration and learning.
- Never compromise on your sleeping hours. Instead lessen your time being spent on sports, entertainment, travelling, part-time job or even for your studies. An adequate hours of sleep ensures enough rest to the mind, hence better concentration and remembrance.
- Pending works and assignments are a big burden and distraction for the mind. Hence, try to finish your tasks as per your time table and schedules.
- It is often felt by many that whenever a task is done in a special way or given extra importance, the results are found to be more positive and encouraging. Hence, attach a special purpose to almost all the tasks that you are responsible for.
- Adopt and follow a simple and positive attitude towards life. Because dishonesty is the most disturbing emotion for the mind. It will also help you to control your bad habits, if any, and also overcome other shortcomings.
- Our mind believes what we make it to believe and feed into it. Hence, feel and act as if you are calm and relaxed before starting any task. It will direct the mind to focus better on the given task.
- Try to choose the right time and atmosphere to start up any new assignment. A good start will ensure good progress. Convenient and suitable timings during the day will vary from person to person. Some people prefer morning hours whereas some prefer late evenings. It also depends on the kind of activity you wish to take up.

Advice: Read this chapter at least three to four times during the day today.

DAY 14

Improve Your Concentration Part – II

The following examples will help you to understand better the concept and importance of concentration. Whenever we watch a good movie starring our favourite actors, we tend to remember the story, the sequences and even the dialogues for a long time. It so happens because we had devoted our full concentration in the movie. Similarly, while playing our favourite game or sport, we generally tend to win the game because we were playing with full, concentration. In both the instances, our mind records even the smallest of details carefully which enables good memory and hence, 'success'.

Exercises to Improve Your Concentration and Focus:

- **Meditation:** Though it is done in various ways around the world, here we will

Today's Date: __ / __ / ____
(Kindly write with a Pencil)

discuss the two ways only which are the most appropriate. It can be done with your eyes closed as well as with your eyes open.

- **Meditation with eyes open:** Sit or stand still and focus your eyes on a fixed object which is 2-3 metres away from you. These objects could be either a wall hanging, a painting or a photo, a black dot measuring a small currency coin, a lamp or a burning candle. The black dot or the lit candle should be preferred.

- **Meditation with eyes closed**: Sit still and straight with legs crossed over each other. Now take a slow, deep breath inside. Now exhale your breath slowly. Repeat it 3-5 times. Keep sitting still, calm and idle. During this time you are neither supposed to talk, do anything or think about anything.

- Just sit idle and silently. Do not try to focus on anything. There is only darkness and peace inside. So, sit still, and feel and enjoy the peace. Now you are one of the few people who have found peace inside yourself and have got connected with it as well.

- Preferably meditate in a silent place where there is minimal or no disturbance of any kind. This is especially important in the initial days of practice. And if there happens to be some kind of noise don't feel disturbed or distracted. Along with your meditation, try to enjoy and absorb this noise. Let it just pass through your mind. Do not ever try to stop it from entering your mind. Because stopping it will only disturb you. So, it is better to let it pass through you. In this way you will be able to keep yourself more relaxed and undisturbed paving the way for eternal bliss.

- Having practised the previous stage, now you have trained your mind to meditate anywhere. It could be either in the bus or train while travelling, waiting at the bus stop, station or even inside a restaurant, at the beach, at the riverside or in a park. You may also concentrate on the sound of waves and a waterfall nearby or get surrounded in the beauty of nature.

- As per your location and convenience, focus your eyes and mind on a certain object which is still, that is which is not moving. It has two great benefits. One is that you are utilising your free time in meditation and increasing your concentration power. And secondly, you are saving yourself from getting bored. Lonliness can provoke you to think negatively as well as you may indulge in some activity which can prove to be injurious to you. Like you may feel the urge to smoke, stare at someone, overeating or even chatting with somebody unnecessarily.

- Meditation is a method to give rest to the mind. Here you are trying to cut off the link of the mind engaged in active thinking, planning or in executing some task. Gradually, with regular practice of 10-15 minutes only everyday, your mind gets used to switching itself off from active thinking and working, and starts feeling relieved and relaxed. Automatically, the time being devoted towards meditation will itself get increased. In that case, you may start using an alarm clock which will alarm you, say after every 20, 30 or 45 minutes.

> **Advice:** Read this chapter at least three or four times during the day. Begin meditation straightaway.

DAY 15

Practice Session - II

Learning by Hit and Trial Method

As we have already discussed earlier, this is another common method of learning. Here learning takes place when you will continuously keep on solving a problem. Repeatedly, keep on trying new ideas and techniques in old and new ways. The more you practise, the better it will get. Moreover, you will also learn how to practise and learn better with every next attempt.

Exercise 1: Prepare a bunch of all the keys that are being used in your house in a common key ring. Lock out all the possible doors and drawers, etc. in your home. Now, start unlocking all the doors and drawers one by one. With the help of your watch, note down the total time taken in a diary. Repeat this activity once every week.

Exercise 2: Locate a big light and switch board having at least 15-20 switches or more in your house, office or a nearby community centre, etc. First, recognise all the respective switches with their respective connections. Switch off all the switches. Now, close your eyes for a minute, take and release a deep breath 3 times and calm your mind down. Now, open your eyes and start switching on the switches. Note down ali the right and wrong attempts in a diary. Repeat the same activity once every week.

In both the exercises above, also judge and mention your performance. The reasons for good performance and the reasons for poor performance on that day. Also, observe the improvements taking place after every month.

Check Your Observation

With the help of the following examples, check and judge your observation power in the first attempt. Only one of the following sentences is correct. Find out and tick the correct one with a light pencil. Also, mark out the mistakes in the other sentences. Kindly find it out for yourself and get it checked by your parents, teachers or any other elder person.

Today's Date: __ / __ / ____
(Kindly write with a Pencil)

Example 1: A. HONESTY IS THE BEST POLICY.

B. HONESTY IS THE BEST POLICY

C. HONESTY IS THE BEST POLICY

D. ONESTY IS THE BEST POLECY

Example 2: A. EARLY TO BED EARLY TO RISE MAKES A MAN HEALTHYY, WEALTHY AND WISE.

B. ERLY TOO BED ERLY TO RISE MAKE A MAN HELTHY, WELTHY AND WISE.

C. EARLY TO BAD EARLY TO RIS MAKES MAN HEELTHY, WEELTHY AND WIS.

D. ARLY TO BED ARLY TO RISE MAKS A MAN HEALTHY, WELLTHY AND WYSE.

Example 3: Check out the lists prepared earlier and make new additions to it.

<table>
<tr><th colspan="4">Detective Stories, Novels or Movies / or Related with Research</th></tr>
<tr><th>S.No.</th><th>Read/Watched</th><th>Reading/Watching</th><th>Planned</th></tr>
<tr><td>1.</td><td></td><td></td><td rowspan="8">Sherlock Holmes
Hardy Boys
Nancy Drew
by Alfred Hitchcock
The Old Fox
Project UFO
Star Trek
James Bond Movies
Discovery Channel,
Animal Planet, etc.
and so on…</td></tr>
<tr><td>2.</td><td></td><td></td></tr>
<tr><td>3.</td><td></td><td></td></tr>
<tr><td>4.</td><td></td><td></td></tr>
<tr><td>5.</td><td></td><td></td></tr>
<tr><td>6.</td><td></td><td></td></tr>
<tr><td>7.</td><td></td><td></td></tr>
<tr><td></td><td></td><td></td></tr>
</table>

Detective works are based on observing the minutest details of the place of crime, activities and emotions of the people related with the event, etc.

Similarly, research and discovery related projects also show the minutest sequence and progress of their research works. Start collecting information about the inventions and discoveries taking place around the world. Try to find out and learn what were the techniques engaged and the various methods adopted by the team involved.

This will train you greatly in your observing, learning and remembering process. This will also make you more cautious in your approach required in general day to day living as well.

Also, enquire from your friends, colleagues or from the nearby bookshop about the detective stories, books or novels available with them, and other such materials related with research and discoveries available with them. Try to borrow such books on returnable basis, at least in the beginning.

Similarly, make enquiries about the TV series or channels.

Other Ways to Improve Observation

Take up any one of the following activities one by one. It will help you in improving your learning, remembering and recalling process.

- Start this with your own room first. Facing an empty or any one of the walls, start writing down all the things, big or small, present in the room without looking back at them. When finished, now check it with all the things present in the room. Repeat this in every month.
- Undertake the above activity when you visit some public office, exhibition, museums, fairs, fetes, hotels and restaurants, etc. Gradually, you will come to know the differences in the thinking of people from the various places visited. It is especially useful for frequent travellers.
- Undertake the activity when you happen to visit your friend or someone in the neighbourhood. Upon return, note down all that you have noticed in their house, room, lobby or terrace. Now check your list when you visit them the next time. Judge your accuracy yourself.
- Count how many steps are there in the stairs of your building, your school, your college or your place of work.
- You may also start noticing and counting the stairs wherever you go. This will help you greatly in enhancing your observation and remembering skills.
- What is the normal time taken to reach the nearest bus stop, park or supermarket if you go walking, by your own vehicle or by some public transport.

- How much time do you generally take to get ready when you are going to your school or office, to play, to the market or when going to attend some party or a function.
- Similarly, how much time do other members in the family take for all the activities stated above.
- Generally what is your heart beat or pulse rate when you have just woken up in the morning, back from school or office, after outdoor sports or work-outs, after cooking or gardening, before and after meals, after prayers or meditation, etc.

Advice: *You may sub-divide the activities as per the availability of your time. Such activities are meant to enhance your memory power but at the same time, it should not disturb your daily schedule.*

What is Memory?

Memory is an important function of the brain without which our existence can come to a standstill. It further comprises three important inter-connected sub-functions. These are Learning, Remembering and Recalling of the information. All these three functions work simultaneously and in tandem with each other. Let us try to understand how all these work.

Each and every moment our mind is recording all the activities that we come across. It could either be by reading, writing, seeing, feeling, smelling, hearing, interacting and so on.

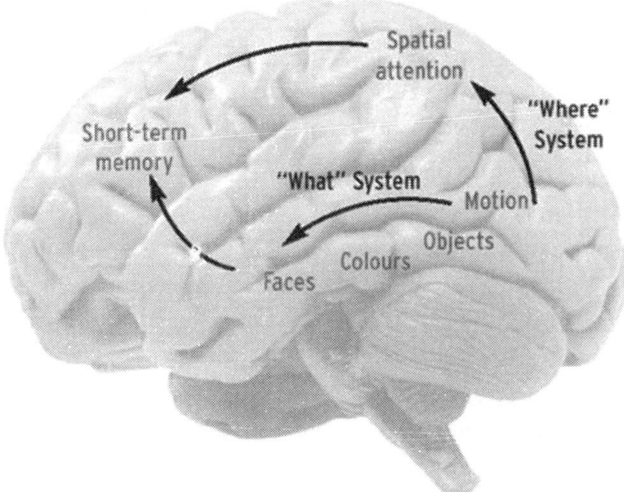

When any activity clicks, it gets noticed or it leaves an impression on the mind and thus *Learning* takes place. When an activity or an event gets repeated or gets stored in the mind it is known as *Retention or Remembering*. It is a natural phenomenon. And lastly, when any such stored information is required the process of *Recalling* is

Today's Date: __ / __ / ____
(Kindly write with a Pencil)

activated by the mind.

Retention of any information can be temporary or for short term and permanent or for longer term. It can also be called short term memory or long term memory respectively. Let us now understand these two characteristics of memory power in a bit more detail.

Short-Term Memory

Any such information that is retained by the mind for a few minutes to a few days and further for a few months only is known as short term memory. In most of the cases we know from the very beginning that the required information will be used in the short term only. Hence, when the stated event happens or by the time the objective gets fulfilled the mind automatically starts to forget all the things gradually, and new things are captured by the mind.

Examples of Short-Term Memory:

- Your travel and lodging details while going on a holiday or for attending a seminar with a delegate out of town. Like your date and timing of travel, your seat no. on the bus, train or airplane you would be travelling by, and similarly for the return journey as well. And your room no. in the hotel or guest house you will be staying and its name.
- Again all the similar details if you happen to visit more than one city during the same trip.
- Subjects and syllabus studied during the whole year is learned, remembered and retained by the mind during the year itself. But, as soon as the final exams are over and we are promoted to the higher class, most of the learned information is lost. And it is taken over by the fresh syllabus. Only the formulas, methods and techniques are retained.
- When we are working on a certain project or assignment the mind learns and remembers all the terms, conditions and directions important to run the project effectively. But as soon as the project is over, gradually our mind tends to forget the details with the passage of time. And, again it is taken over by the new guidelines of the new assignment.

Long-Term Memory

Any such information that is retained by the mind for a longer duration extending from a few years to the entire lifetime of a person is known as long term memory. These are the formulas and techniques that we generally learn during our studying years or while working in the professional domain as well. As per our way of thinking and attitude towards life, we constantly give directions to our subconscious mind about the importance of the information we are coming across, and accordingly our mind remembers those things for a longer duration. All such things once learnt may be applied for several times in your life.

Examples of Long-Term Memory:

- Formulas of mathematics, grammar, punctuation and tenses of any language; laws of scientific or fundamentals of physics and chemistry, and so on.
- Remembering birthday and anniversary dates of your near and dear ones. It helps in maintaining good relationships all around.
- Learning for yourself or by simply observing other people repairing household goods or even tending to small problems with your vehicles. These could be as simple as fixing the blades of a juicer or grinder in the kitchen, mending the fuse in the electricity box of your house, tightening of loose wires in the plug or switch, soldering the broken wires of your electric iron, changing the punctured wheel of your motorbike or car, and so on.
- Cooking food starting with simple things first. Like boiling of water or milk for preparing tea or coffee, and gradually, adding other ingredients to prepare the desired dish or beverage. Butter toast, sandwich and omelette is a very common breakfast which is eaten and cherished worldwide.
- Learning good etiquettes, manners and behaviour is also an important part of our daily life. These are mostly learnt by good observation and is useful throughout life.

Exercises for the Day:

- To properly understand what all has been told above, kindly prepare two separate lists. One list will be for the past and the other will be for the future.
- Now divide both these two lists further into two sections each namely short term and long term.

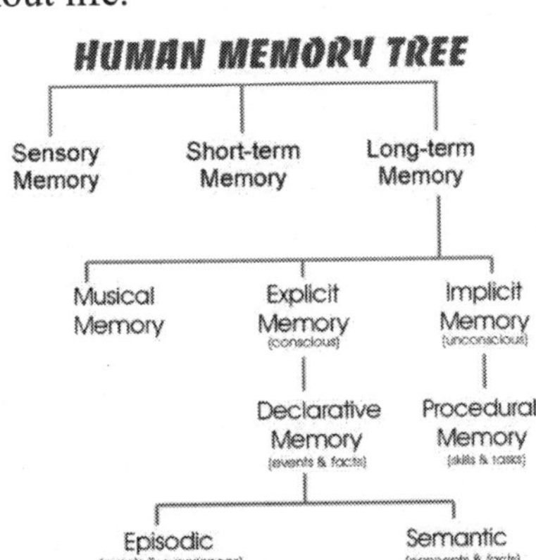

- In the Past list – long-term section, write down all the events, activities and information that you remember from your childhood and teenage days, e.g. your first day at school or the day you went to buy your first bicycle or skates; when you stood first in your class or when you won the race on sports day; your first love and so on.
- In the Past list – short-term section, write down all the events, activities and information that you remember from the recent past, e.g. a new friend or colleague whose friendship you like the most; or you were promoted, given a raise in salary or awarded a medal for your accomplishments; your decision to buy a car on your previous birthday, and so on.
- In the Future list – long-term section, write down all the events, activities and information that you feel would be required for the rest of your life, e.g. keep safely all the photographs of yourself and your family clicked during family functions; a big desk diary to note down the important events of life like birthdays and anniversaries of family members and friends or colleagues, etc. and so on.
- In the Future list – short-term section, write down all the events, activities and information that you feel would be required for a few months only., e.g. carefully retain the documents and bills of the new TV and juicer purchased for free repairs during the warranty period; other documents of incomes and major purchases which could be required by the taxmen, and so on.

FROM THE PAST		
S.No.	**LONG-TERM**	**SHORT-TERM**
1.	first day at school	a new friend met last year
2.	parents giving in to my persistent demand for a new bicycle	migrating to another city for studies only
3.		

FOR THE FUTURE		
S.No.	**LONG-TERM**	**SHORT-TERM**
1.	construction of own dream house	a small hike in salary for good work done

2.	admission to MBA with weekend classes	scholarship granted for higher studies
3.		

You can keep adding and re-arranging the list as per your liking and convenience on a regular basis as well. But try to complete a major part of these lists today itself to give it a good start. This will help you a lot to understand the working of our minds.

Written down approach is the best technique to increase your memory power. If you can develop the habit of writing down the important things of life in a diary, I can assure you that you will soon develop a memory that would be at par with the most intellectual people of this world. So, start today itself. Maintain a good quality desk diary for long-term usage and a small pocket diary for short-term usage. You will yourself feel the difference in a few days from today onwards.

Advice: Read this chapter at least three to four times during the day today.

How to Overcome 'Forgetting'? DAY 17

What is Forgetting?

Inability of the mind to recall information is known as 'forgetting'. It may either be complete or partial. Forgetting Completely happens when we are not at all able to recall things which we may have used or come across earlier. Forgetting Partially means when we are able to recall some part of the things, but not everything.

We will try to understand these two types of 'forgetting' with the help of the following examples:

- Forgetting Completely happens when we fail to recall something we had read or learnt earlier or visited a place like a temple, a museum or a picnic spot. We may also fail to recognise a school time friend or an accomplice with whom we had worked previously on an assignment.
- Forgetting Partially takes place when we come across a person and recognise him as well but are not able to recall his name or as to where we had met earlier. This is a very common instance of partial recognition.
- Forgetting takes place in a third way also. When some other person recognises us and we are not able to recognise him. But when that person uses certain references with respect to some common friends or the places we had visited together or some

Today's Date: __ / __ / ____
(Kindly write with a Pencil)

other moments, we both had enjoyed together during the execution of a project, etc., we start recognising that person.

Importance of Forgetting

As we all know that our mind comes across numerous activities and things every moment. We also know that learning, remembering and forgetting is a naturally occurring continuous process. Forgetting old things is as important as learning new things.

Forgetting declutters the mind, eliminates and automatically deletes various subjects and issues in due course of time. Forgetting empties the space required for storing fresh information. Moreover, it also helps to avoid any such unimportant things from interfering in our day-to-day life, and helps in keeping the good memory intact.

Hence, it becomes utmost important for us to train our minds in such a way that it automatically filters and forgets all the irrelevant things from the mind, and makes more space for new and other important things. This is the basic difference between intellectuals and slow learners. All intellectuals and learned people have two things in common. One is, that they have trained their minds to learn faster and filter the trivial things successfully. And secondly, that they work harder and practise more than other people till the time they have properly learned the requisite skills.

Reasons for Forgetting

There are numerous reasons for forgetting. But with little efforts and careful handling of the affairs of daily routine life, the habit of forgetting and poor remembrance can be taken care of very effectively. It is not so difficult as has been considered by many. Children often tend to forget many small things during their examination days. Candidates appearing for an interview suddenly develop cold feet, start trembling or sweating. Psychologists have pointed out the following reasons:

- Disinterest, disregard or neglect towards a certain subject or issue often results into poor remembrance and hence, weaker recalling.
- Non-willingness to remember something.
- Studying and understanding a subject matter with little interest, lack of proper focus and without complete concentration.
- Continuous worries, tensions and stress also take a great toll on the ability of the mind to properly remember things.
- Peer pressure as well as continuous pressure by parents to excel in exams and competitions also burden and worry children un-

necessarily about the outcome of their exams and their future.

- Children are innocent and soft-hearted. Already under immense pressure in higher classes and preparation days, any uneventful mis-happening or demise of a family member is a big jolt for them.
- Prolonged illness or getting hurt in an accident also results into lack of proper concentration in preparations as well as during exams.
- Disturbed atmosphere of the family also adversely affects the concentration and understanding of children.
- Hereditary factors also influence children towards pursuing certain interests. If such interests are towards activities other than studies, then they are likely to have little interest in studies and hence, weaker remembrance.

In a nutshell, lack of interest and concentration in studies or certain subjects is likely to result into low understanding, low remembrance and hence, weaker retrieval of information.

Avoid Forgetting

Sometimes some children are found to be repenting about their weak memory power, inability to learn thoroughly and often forgetting their lessons. It is much found to see during the preparation and exam days. Here are some tips for better learning and good memory which put some students ahead of others. These are:

- It is utmost important that how these few days are spent. It makes a lot of difference in learning and scoring well. If you have been good throughout the year but got nervous or carefree during these days then all your efforts are going to get wasted. So, be cautious and alert in your approach towards your preparations.
- Do not overexert yourself or put extra load on your mind. Every person has his own unique set of mental capacities of working,

learning and remembering. The actual problem begins when we start comparing and competing ourselves with others.

- Take frequent breaks in between studies. Try to relax your brain. Give it what it wants. It will help you save a lot of your quality time and efforts.
- Such breaks should not exceed for more than 10-15 minutes maximum. It could include a short nap with eyes closed and lying down straight; or enjoying some form of music or songs of choice; walking on fresh, clean and green grass; a quick bath or washing face, hands and feet a number of times; drinking plain water as much as possible to keep the body hydrated and for better working of the nervous system, thus keeping mental fatigue away, etc.
- But such breaks should not include watching TV or useless internet surfing; roaming or unnecessary chatting with friends; munching spicy or oily food, snacks or fast food; overeating in any way to check mood swings; or any such activity which keeps you away from your books for a longer duration.
- It is a myth that beverages like tea, coffee and cold drinks, etc. help to keep the mind fresh and alert for a longer duration. Although it gives a push to the nervous system but it is for a few minutes only. Instead, it dehydrates the body which causes more harm than good. Many a time, these drinks also cause heartburn, acidity, mouth sores and stomach ulcers for some. So, it should be avoided or used limitedly.
- Intake of tobacco products, cigarette smoking and consuming alcohol is a big 'NO', particularly during the school and college going days. This time is very crucial for the optimum development of the mind and body alike. These products can severely damage the proper growth and functioning of the mind.
- Try keeping your haircut as short as possible, especially for men. The shorter the better. It is good in keeping the mind fresh and calm naturally. At this time, it is more important to concentrate on studies, score well and be appreciated for your hard work and sincerity. In ancient India, students were kept bald head with only a small nape at the upper back of their heads during their sudent period.
- Once, the momentum of studies picks up, the understanding and learning of respective subjects begins getting better which results

into good remembrance also, and gradually, self-confidence also starts building up. It further induces courage and motivation to work harder, score well and be meritorious.

- Do not worry much about the results, the outcome or about the future but just concentrate more on studying at the moment. Take one subject at a time. Plan your time-table yourself and divide it appropriately among different subjects, projects and other activities.

Improve Learning & Reduce Forgetting

The following suggestions will guide you to improve your learning capacities and simultaneously minimise the factors responsible for forgetting things that have relevance for us. These are:

Interest and Eagerness to Learn

This is a natural phenomenon that the mind grasps and learns faster with more accuracy when the person is eager to learn something. The mental energies work in such a way that the mind retains the things better when there is an eagerness to learn.

Concentration

At many times, our mind becomes a great wanderer besides being lazy at the time of putting efforts and hard work into any work. So in such situations, the mind has to be controlled effectively, motivated and its energies directed towards the work only. For this to happen, a concentrated effort is required to bear the desired results.

Pictorials and Examples

Our mind learns those things faster which are presented to it by way of pictures, diagrams, video clips or by citing some examples or other interesting quotations. Students in the primary classes are taught in this way because their learning has just started.

But when there are no such things provided along with your study material, try to create your own by using your imagination. Such things take far lesser time in understanding and the time of recalling things also gets reduced. People are also able to remember such things for longer durations.

For example, a mouse is being chased by a cat, the cat is being chased by a dog and the dog is being chased by a man with a stick. By imagination, if we try to visualise the scenario then it would become quite easy for us to remember the story, and we would be able to relate and recall it easily at a future date.

Relating and Logical Thinking

It becomes much easier for the mind to remember things when the newer things get related with the older things learnt earlier. Such kind of connections appears when the mind is able to form logical bonding between the new and the older data. In this way also, the mind is able to remember things for longer durations with better accuracy and faster recalling.

When you start understanding the logic of any subject matter, it becomes easier to remember it also. Similarly, when you also begin understanding the interconnections of various subjects of your syllabus as well as various issues of your life, the remembering process gets logical and easier. Hence, always try to make a connection.

Attraction towards the Unusual

Our mind gets greatly attracted towards something happening in an unusual way and also all the new things that it comes across. Some examples are – a new discovery or invention; a new design or experiment; an old song being sung in a new and different way; a person using his left hand for playing a difficult game, eating and for other activities; a woman driving a heavy commercial vehicle; a person riding a bicycle with his face backwards or with folding hands, and so on. Such things remain in the mind for longer durations.

Synonyms and Antonyms

Words having similar meanings are known as *synonyms,* whereas words having opposite meanings are known as *antonyms*. This is also an easy way to memorise things.

Examples of a few synonyms are: happy-joyful, sad-worried, climb-ascend, decline-descend, getting-receiving, giving-parting, and so on.

Examples of a few antonyms are: hot-cold, winter-summer, in-out, high-low, rich-poor, good-bad, happy-sad, hard working-lazy, and so on.

Short Intervals and Rest

Always ensure for your mind adequate rest and relaxation by way of frequent intervals in between. This greatly enhances remembrance and storing of things that have been studied and learnt up to such breaks. Such intervals give due rest to the mind which in turn increases its capacity manifold for further learning and remembering.

Music

Playing some light music along with your studies or while working helps to keep the mind relaxed as well as focused on the task at hand. It also helps to cut out on any other kind of disturbances caused by noises in the vicinity. You may choose the music of your liking so that it helps you to maintain your concentration. You may, also try playing a musical instrument in your free time to de-stress yourself.

Sub-division of Bigger Topics

Though it is better to study and finish a topic in a single sitting but in case of bigger lessons it is advisable to divide such topics into two or more sections or sittings. For this, first a general reading should be carried out and thereafter such topics should be divided as per their relevance and applicability. In this way the topics are learnt more effectively while maintaining the connectivity with the main topic as well.

Repetition and Practice

This is the most common and the most effective method known and followed worldwide. Learning, remembering and its retention becomes much easier and better when something is repeated. The more it is practised, the better it gets with every repetition.

Repetition of a subject matter becomes utmost important when we wish to retain the information in the same way we intend it to use it later. And, every repetition takes lesser efforts and lesser time to repeat the said subject matter and its learning. Our mind functions better in this way.

Repetition may be done either by reading, writing, listening or by practising if it is of practical nature. In all the four methods, the verbal repetition done along with can be carried out slowly in the mind or in high tone. It is adviced to be done in a higher volume, because that way the remembrance and its retention increases manifold.

For example, students of the primary school are often found to be repeating their texts in high tone. This is the best method especially for those who have just begun their education. It is also very much suitable for children who are slow learners or for those who are not able to concentrate well in their studies. Also, very effective during the examination time when the pressure is high and the time is limited to cover the study material.

Here is a very common example of the visible effects of repetition. You must have come across several tracks used by people as a shortcut from the main road. Such tracks get formed automatically later on in due course of time when used repeatedly. Similarly, a hollow is formed on the ground or even a hard stone where water falls continuously in the form of droplets or as a regular flow. Hence, repetition is always good for learning and good remembering.

Inspiration and Motivation

When a person is inspired or gets motivated to do something, then the subconscious mind becomes active and takes due interest in the activities. This further enables faster learning, better remembrance and good retention as well as faster recalling in the future.

> **Advice:** Read this chapter at least three to four times during the day today. It will help you to differentiate the different forms of the learning and remembering systems undertaken by the mind.

***

DAY 18

Improve Your Memory Part – I

Today, we will test your memory by undertaking a small test. This test has been sub-divided into smaller and different parts. Though the previous chapters would have certainly given you a fair idea about the way your mind works, after taking the following tests, you will come to know the actual working capacity of your mind. This will further help you to get better in your daily approach.

Exercise 1: Some words are mentioned below. You have to read slowly and observe these words, understand them and relate them in your mind. After finishing, close the book and write them on a piece of paper. Do not forget to mention today's date before you start writing.

Banana, Moon, Bear, Mouse, Galaxy, Biscuits, Butterfly, Chair, Internet, Pen, Cow, Giraffe, Tomato, Pencil, Planets, Chalk, Rabbit, Potato, Spaceship, Astronaut, Zebra, Salt, Peacock, Rocket, Emails, Tiger, Notebook, Sugar, Jupiter, Almonds, Earth, Strawberry, Burger, Mobile Aeroplane, French, Fries, Ticket, Laptop.

(Tip: Rearrange all the above words in different columns as per their similarities.)

S.No.	I	II	III	IV
1.	Apple	Fish	Stars	Table
2.	Banana	Bear	Galaxy	Chair
3.	Tomato	Giraffe	Planets	Chalk
4.	Potato	Zebra	Moon	Pencil
5.	Strawberry	Rabbit	Spaceship	Notebook
6.	Biscuits	Mouse	Astronaut	Pen
7.	Sugar	Butterfly	Rocket	Laptop
8.	Salt	Peacock	Aeroplane	Internet
9.	French Fries	Tiger	Jupiter	Mobile
10.	Burger	Cow	Earth	E-mails
11.	Almonds		Ticket	

Exercise 2: Below are mentioned some birthday dates of important and lovely people in my life. Good people will always keep on getting added to this list. I will suggest you some easy ways to remember them. Accordingly, you have to prepare your own list. Kindly follow the tips. It helps to maintain good relationships with people.

Mr.Varinder Aggarwal	24 January 19	Mr.Vimal Jaitly	9 January 1974
Mr.Arun Sagar	20 November1968	Mr.Piyush Aggarwal	6 February 1977
Mr.Vishal Mani	15 April 1975	Mr.Harinder Singh	24 January 1954
Dr.P.K.Gupta	22 October 1956	Mrs.Mamo Devi	2 January 19
Baby Ananya Singhal	2 August 2011	Mr.Aditya Gupta	2 February 1989
Miss Vibhu Aggarwal	9 March 1995	Mrs.Madhubala Nagar	9 February 19
Mr.Sanjay Singhal	5 January 1973	Mr.Sunil Madan	7 March 1961
Mr.Ashish Goel	2 February 1982	Mr.Raman Nagpal	1 March 1975
Mr.Raman Dua	25 September 1979	Miss Nikita Gupta	21 October 19
Mrs.Ranjana Aggarwal	18 April 19	Mr.Satpal Singh Bhatia	25 May 1961
Mr.Gautam Singhal	12 March 1981	Mr.Sanjay Verma	1 July 1971
Baby Diksha Bajaj	5 May 2005	Mr.Sunil Wadhwa	18 December 19

Mr.Avnish Gupta	1 May 1987	Mr.Abhishek Saxena	5 July 1980
Mr.Ranjeet Singh Bisht	14 June 1980	Mr.Naresh Kumar Bajaj	25 May 1979
Mr.Satish Kumar Aggarwal	25 June 1974	Mrs.Neha Chandel	27 July 19
Mr.Vikas Gupta	8 July 1985	Mr.Ayush Aggarwal	3 August 1996
Mr.Sanjay Dhama	1 July 1973	Mr.Karan Chawla	12 August 1984
Mr.Manjeet Singh Bisht	30 August 1978	Mr.Anil Kumar Mahajan	25 October 1965
Mr.Umesh Sharma	20 December 1956	Mr.Lalit Saini	22 September 1981
Mr.Kamal Kant Kalra	4 December 1979	Dr.Himanshi Verma	21 December 19
Mr.Chandan Pawar	23 September 1975	Mr.Gaurav Chawla	31 October 1979
Mr.Girish Bhandari	26 August 19	Dr.Kamal Kumar Kapoor	2 December 1974
Mr.Sanjeev Kumar	27 December 19	Mr.Amit Girdhar	15 January 1975
Mr.Amit Saxena	31 December 1983	Mr.Vikram Sharma	27 December 1975
Mr.Rajinder S Ahluwalia	26 August 1966	Mr.Suresh Kumar Garg	15 March 1957
Mr.Nitin Gupta	1 December 19	Mr.Prashant Kapoor	6 November 1995
Mr.Amit Puri	1 April 1978	Anil Kumar	14 April 1975

Tip 1: Make a month-wise list of the above data for better remembrance and faster recalling. Write it in ascending order.

Tip 2: Birthdays can also be easily remembered when the dates, months and years are similar with your own date of birth, e.g. all people whose date starts with 24 or falls in January, like mine. There is some matching by way of thinking or similar wavelength, -- birth numbers are divisible by: (3) 3,6,9,12,... (4) 4,8,12,… (6) 6,12,18,24,…etc. -- total or basic numbers are the same, e.g. (1,10,19-1+9=10=1+0=1,28) (3,12,21,30), (4,13,22,31), (5,14,23), (8,17,24), … and so on.

Tip 3: The best proven way is to greet them on their special days every year. It could be by emails, message, by calling, by sending a card by post or an e-card, or presenting them a bouquet of flowers, a gift, chocolates or sweets, etc. Your relationship will get special with each passing year…

JANUARY		FEBRUARY	
Mrs.Mamo Devi	2 January 19	Mr.Aditya Gupta	2 February 1989
Mr.Sanjay Singhal	5 January 1973	Mr.Ashish Goel	2 February 1982
Mr.Vimal Jaitly	9 January 1974	Mr.Piyush Aggarwal	6 February 1977
Mr.Amit Girdhar	15 January 1975	Mrs.Madhubala Nagar	9 February 19
Mr.Varinder Aggarwal	24 January 19		
Mr.Harinder Singh	24 January 1954		
Mr.Pushpesh Dhingra	24 January 1973		
MARCH		**APRIL**	
Mr.Raman Nagpal	1 March 1975	Mr.Amit Puri	1 April 1978
Mr.Sunil Madan	7 March 1961	Anil Kumar	14 April 1975
Miss Vibhu Aggarwal	9 March 1995	Mr.Vishal Mani	15 April 1975
Mr.Gautam Singhal	12 March 1981	Mrs.Ranjana Aggarwal	18 April 19
Mr.Suresh Kumar Garg	15 March 1957		
MAY		**JUNE**	
Mr.Avnish Gupta	1 May 1987	Mr.Ranjeet Singh Bisht	14 June 1980
Baby Diksha Bajaj	5 May 2005	Mr.Satish Kumar Aggarwal	25 June 1974
Mr.Satpal Singh Bhatia	25 May 1961		
Mr.Naresh Kumar Bajaj	25 May 1979		
JULY		**AUGUST**	
Mr.Sanjay Verma	1 July 1971	Baby Ananya Singhal	2 August 2011
Mr.Sanjay Dhama	1 July 1973	Mr.Ayush Aggarwal	3 August 1996
Mr.Abhishek Saxena	5 July 1980	Mr.Karan Chawla	12 August 1984
Mrs.Neha Chandel	27 July 19	Mr.Rajinder S Ahluwalia	26 August 1966
Mr.Vikas Gupta	8 July 1985	Mr.Girish Bhandari	26 August 19
		Mr.Manjeet Singh Bisht	30 August 1978
SEPTEMBER		**OCTOBER**	
Mr.Lalit Saini	22 September 1981	Miss Nikita Gupta	21 October 19
Mr.Chandan Pawar	23 September 1975	Dr.P.K.Gupta	22 October 1956
Mr.Raman Dua	25 September 1979	Mr.Anil Kumar Mahajan	25 October 1965
		Mr.Gaurav Chawla	31 October 1979
NOVEMBER		**DECEMBER**	
Mr.Prashant Kapoor	6 November 1995	Mr.Nitin Gupta	1 December 19
Mr.Arun Sagar	20 November1968	Dr.Kamal Kumar Kapoor	2 December 1974

Mr.Rajeev Goyal	26 November 1984	Mr.Kamal Kant Kalra	4 December 1979
		Mr.Sunil Wadhwa	18 December 19
		Mr.Umesh Sharma	20 December 1956
		Dr.Himanshi Verma	21 December 1973
		Mr.Sanjeev Kumar	27 December 19
		Mr.Vikram Sharma	27 December 1975
		Mr.Amit Saxena	31 December 1983

DAY 19

Improve Your Memory Part - II

Formation of Different Words

Using the letters mentioned below, create as many words as possible. You have to use all the different letters only once to form the words. So, get started.

Exercise 1: U A B T I R T S E

BETTER	BET	BEST	BITTER	BUTTER	BAT
BED	BELT	TEST	TESTER	TESTED	TREAT
SET	SETTLE	SEAT	...	...	...

Exercise 2: C E H T S R A

CARE	RACE	EAR	ACE	ARE	CAR
CASH	ASH	HAS	HAT	RAT	CAT
TEAR	SEAT	TEACH	...	...	...

Exercise 3: O T G A E S

GOAT	GATE	TAG	STAGE	STAG	SAGE
GET	ATE	GOT	OATS	...	...

Example 4: Find different eatables among the following bunch of words and encircle or highlight them. These are written as – straight forward, straight down or straight diagonally down. You may note them separately as well.

Today's Date: __ / __ / ____
(Kindly write with a Pencil)

A	P	B	E	T	C	V	X	Z	B	F	I	T	O	P	O	S	A	A	L
C	A	T	F	I	S	H	K	U	P	T	Y	O	G	U	R	T	Y	R	I
Y	N	W	B	C	U	I	P	M	L	I	C	A	S	V	Z	W	O	U	N
N	C	Y	B	A	N	A	N	A	R	O	B	S	P	I	N	A	C	H	O
Q	A	X	U	R	P	S	P	A	G	H	E	T	T	I	I	F	T	A	P
A	K	E	R	V	B	J	L	P	O	I	R	R	U	S	P	E	R	M	S
V	E	G	G	S	M	I	J	N	L	C	T	P	N	M	S	R	I	B	E
E	S	I	E	B	P	E	A	C	H	E	S	O	T	E	P	S	U	U	K
A	S	N	R	P	A	I	R	A	G	U	T	S	R	I	O	F	L	R	E
P	L	G	U	T	O	N	Z	E	P	T	R	U	I	N	T	E	A	G	L
E	V	E	U	L	T	U	R	Z	E	R	A	N	C	G	A	T	I	E	B
Y	E	R	E	L	L	O	W	P	A	U	W	H	E	A	T	R	P	R	E
L	A	M	U	F	F	I	N	S	B	L	B	E	A	R	O	L	Y	B	I
R	D	E	N	W	I	N	E	J	O	O	E	Y	T	H	E	D	A	Y	W
I	T	H	M	E	S	O	K	A	Y	B	R	E	W	I	L	M	E	A	G
A	I	N	O	C	H	I	P	S	F	O	R	A	A	L	M	O	N	D	S
X	H	E	N	H	B	L	E	A	C	H	Y	Y	N	E	W	F	O	L	D
G	A	R	L	I	C	R	A	N	E	A	G	L	E	G	D	Y	O	W	L
A	R	E	B	C	D	U	R	E	S	T	O	F	B	R	E	A	D	E	O
U	W	T	H	K	A	M	S	N	P	C	H	E	E	S	E	G	L	I	V
G	R	A	P	E	S	I	N	G	K	I	U	B	E	H	O	N	E	Y	L
E	W	A	L	N	U	T	S	A	L	T	T	V	F	E	A	S	S	T	Y

Some of them are:

Bread, Eggs, Banana, Pears, Beef, Pizza, Apple, and so on…

……………………………………………………………………………………………

……………………………………………………………………………………………

(Kindly use a soft pencil)

Advice: Practise, practise, and practise…

***

Code Language

Code language is a method of remembering things in an easier and comfortable way. 'Code' here means to remember things by some other name or sign. Many people use this method to remember and differentiate between different things. It could differ from person to person. Each and every person has his/her own way of thinking. You may refer other person's code, but it is better to develop your own. Let us see this through an example.

Example 1: Following is a code language for numbers that are written in words. It is just an example to make you understand. You may create your own. The idea is to remember the numbers in a simpler way by relating them with something else. You will observe a kind of tuning or rhythm in the numbers and their codes.

Numbers	Numbers in Words	Codes for Numbers
1	ONE	RUN
2	TWO	WHO
3	THREE	TREE
4	FOUR	FLOOR
5	FIVE	HIVE
6	SIX	FIX
7	SEVEN	HEAVEN
8	EIGHT	WEIGHT
9	NINE	MINE
10	TEN	DEN
11	ELEVEN	EVEN
12	TWELVE	SHELVE
13	THIRTEEN	HURTING

Today's Date: __ / __ / ____
(Kindly write with a Pencil)

14	FOURTEEN	FLOORING
15	FIFTEEN	LIFTING
16	SIXTEEN	SEEING
17	SEVENTEEN	EVENING
18	EIGHTEEN	EIGHT LANE (ROAD)
19	NINETEEN	NINTH INN
20	TWENTY	HEFTY

Exercise 1: Now let us practise the above code language. Match the words and numbers with their respective codes by drawing lines.

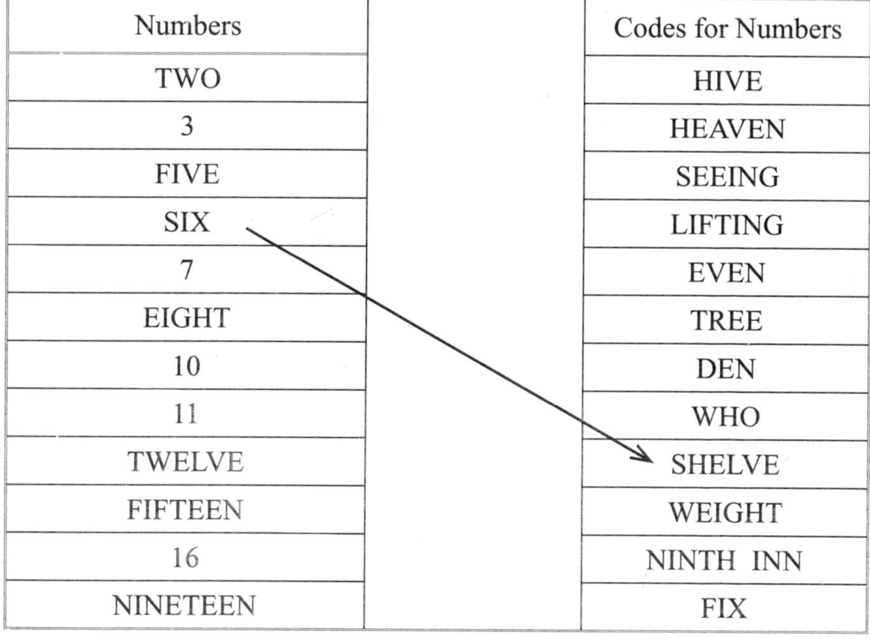

Numbers		Codes for Numbers
TWO		HIVE
3		HEAVEN
FIVE		SEEING
SIX		LIFTING
7		EVEN
EIGHT		TREE
10		DEN
11		WHO
TWELVE		SHELVE
FIFTEEN		WEIGHT
16		NINTH INN
NINETEEN		FIX

Example 2: Another way of coding numbers.

Z=0, A=1, B=2, C=3, D=4, E=5, F=6, G=7, H=8, I=9.

Numbers	Codes	Numbers	Codes	Numbers	Codes
21	BA	36	CF	51	EA
22	BB	37	CG	52	EB
23	BC	38	CH	53	EC
24	BD	39	CI	54	ED

25	BE	40	DZ	55	EE
26	BF	41	DA	56	EF
27	BG	42	DB	57	EG
28	BH	43	DC	58	EH
29	BI	44	DD	59	EI
30	CZ	45	DE	60	FZ
31	CA	46	DF	61	FA
32	CB	47	DG	62	FB
33	CC	48	DH	63	FC
34	CD	49	DI	64	FD
35	CE	50	EZ	65	FE

You can further relate these codes as initials in the following ways:

BA = British Airways BF = Boy Friend CG = College Girl
CA = Chartered Accountant CD = CD Player FD = Fixed Deposit
BE = Bachelor of Electronics DA = Delhi Airport EZ = Easy
CH = Holiday in Canada FA = First Attempt … and so on.

Example 3: Relate the things of your shopping list with something. The more logical the connection, the better remembrance you can have.

SHOPPING LIST	CODE	REMINDED BY
MIRROR	My Beautiful Hair (as seen every morning)	Reflection in a Car Mirror
DETERGENT	Feeling of Freshness	Shining White Shirt of a Passerby
TOOTHBRUSH	My Shining Teeth	Dirty Teeth of the Shopkeeper
TEA	My Favourite Aroma Every Morning	Grocery Shop Owner Sipping Tea

CHOCOLATE	Tasty My Favourite Sweet	A Child Eating Chocolate on the Way
SHARPENER	Sharp Pencil Tip	Broken Tip of My Pencil in the Geometry Box
MEDICINE	Lifeline of My Grandfather	An Elderly Coughing Nearby
MOBILE BATTERY CHARGER	I Cannot do without My Mobile	Low Battery Beep by the Mobile Handset

Tips for Students

Students should take due note that it is very important to have good memory power to excel in their studies as well as be meritorious in their exams. The format of question papers has changed drastically over the years from a few big questions to only small and multiple objective type questions. It is followed almost in all competitive exams.

The new format now requires more sharpness and alertness of the mind. It also requires very good speed and accuracy to attempt all the questions correctly. The marking now depends on the increased number of questions answered and hence, the margin of scoring is thin amongst students. Any small mistake can leave them behind others. Competition is increasing day by day with the increase in syllabus. It further exerts pressure on the mind and its effective working.

Besides exams and competitions, sharp memory is a must to be successful in other spheres of life as well. All the great and successful people in the world possess special qualities of great memory power and instant decision making abilities.

Psychologists believe that most of the students have similar kind of average thinking capacity. There are only a few who are either slow in thinking or possess extremely good intellect and some are even outstanding. Doctors are of the opinion that impatience, worries, work-overload and stress have severely affected the efficiency of the memory power. Monotonous schedules and long working hours along with lonliness and boredom is depleting good and efficient memory of people.

We generally tend to forget those issues which are of lesser importance or we don't want to remember them anymore. But we never forget all those things and events which are of our interest and our liking. Psychologists have pointed out that there is a very strong connection between the issues of our interest with our memory and remembrance.

Today's Date: __ / __ / ____
(Kindly write with a Pencil)

Children with sharp intellect is the result of their interest and concentration in the said subjects as well as their good observation, and students scoring lesser marks or failing miserably in exams show their lack of interest in studies. Having good memory power is a sign of being more thoughtful and more intelligent. So, it is important to have good memory in order to have a good personality also. That is why forgetful students are not able to remember their lessons properly, also tend to forget other important things of their routine life.

Following are some methods which will help in maintaining and enhancing good learning and memory power:

Focus on Your Goals

Setting goals is the first and foremost step towards planning and working to be meritorious. When all of our senses are focussed on our goals along with enthusiasm then it becomes easier to devote time and efforts in preparing for the exams. Enthusiasm works in the most positive way in uplifting the mood. An enthusiastic person will always be energetic and active in his thinking and performance. Such an approach is bound to yield the much desired results.

Develop Interest in Studies

Taking deep interest in studies ensures good understanding of the lessons and hence, results into better remembrance. Being interested in a subject initiates the basic motivation towards it. It further facilitates in studying it thoroughly. It becomes rather easier to learn it by understanding the basics of the said subject. It further helps to study it continuously for more hours altogether which makes more sense towards the current topic. It also helps in getting more attached with the books and avoids in drifting away towards other useless activities. Such inclination towards studies directs children on the path of becoming meritorious as well as being successful in their careers.

Keep Your Mind Calm

Mind is the most complex machine and the most capable natural super-computer. It records, undertakes and effectively executes numerous functions every second. The mind works continuously without any rest or break even for split of a second. An important fact to consider is that what we get as an outcome from the mind is the direct result of our thoughts and actions. We will get good results if we feed good and positive thoughts into our mind, and we will get negative results if we feed bad or negative thoughts into our mind.

Such a detailed description of the functioning of the mind is given only to emphasize on its capability, functioning and utility. Hence, it becomes our inherent duty to use it most effectively towards the development of our skills and talents. It will further help us to study and learn our syllabus better, and perform with optimum levels during the exams enabling us to be meritorious.

The mind should always be kept happy and joyous, relaxed and calm which provides it a kind of rest in itself. Otherwise, it will directly impact its capability and working in a very negative way. And, whenever the mind is relaxed the learning and remembering gets more easy and effective. Also, develop a habit a noting down all your important matters in a diary. Gradually, this habit will help you in relaxing your mind. It will also help to ease much of the pressure which was earlier being handled by the mind. In turn, now you will start feeling more refreshed day by day.

Understand the Subject Matter First

Learning and remembering happens smoothly whenever a subject is read with its proper understanding. And whenever we need any such information the data appears to be readily available. We need not put any extra pressure on the mind. Whereas when we try to learn things by repetition only, it appears to have been learnt, but for the time being only. Later on, we are not able to remember or recall properly what we had learnt at that time. Moreover, we are also not able to co-relate it with other related topics, and hence start to lag behind others. Therefore, understanding the meaning of the subject matter is very important.

Think and Evaluate Deeply

Always think and evaluate the topics you read, study and come across. It may be by way of print or electronic medium, seminars, presentations, lectures, debates or even simple interactions. This greatly helps in enhancing the fertility of the mind. It makes it quite easier to understand, learn and remember the subject matter as well as the logic behind it. Whenever the logic is clear then there are no doubts of any kind in the mind. And the learning process gets simplified.

Techniques for Good Remembrance

Besides the above mentioned methods, you should also practise the other methods and techniques that have been suggested elsewhere in this book. It would also be better to repeat them some days prior to your exams. This will help you to take control and train your mind. You will further be helped by it from getting distracted and therefore, fully concentrate on your studies only. In this way, you can ensure yourself not only good marks but also in getting ahead of others.

Improve Memory by Interaction

Talking or discussing a topic with others helps in enhancing knowledge of the subject matter. It also aids in better learning and remembrance. Here the idea again is repetition. Mere reading, watching or listening could be boring at many times but having a conversation with others could prove to be very beneficial. It could turn out to be even more interesting with whom you share similar wavelength.

The sages and wise men have always recommended to have healthy discussions and share good noble thoughts only with others. In this way it creates a positive environment all around. Positive vibrations stimulate the mind more and in turn, it churns out good and joyous feelings for everyone.

Own Creativity

A person's creativity helps him in understanding and relating with the subject matter in his own way which is more suitable to his mindset. That is why studying something with focus and concentration helps more. When the mind is relaxed and happy then creativity works at its optimum level, hence, again better remembrance.

Maintain a Diary

A diary is a very effective tool which helps keep the mind relaxed by noting down the routine information in the form of tips. It relieves the mind from extra pressures due the to daily chores faced at home or at the office.

Instead, the mind should be used to store those information only which is important for the normal functioning of your professional and personal lives. During exams, a person is dependent only on the capability of his mind. His performance would depend only on how effectively he has trained his mind towards learning and remembering his syllabus.

Read and Repeat Aloud

Learning and remembering is done by reading, writing and listening. So, when reading is in process, it should be loud enough to be heard clearly. In this way, the mind grasps it more easily. Similarly, when you are engaged in writing something, it should also be read aloud so that the mind hears it clearly. Thus the learning and remembering process becomes more effective and thorough.

Finish a Topic in Single Sitting

Students should try to study and finish a whole chapter in one sitting only. It makes more sense and relates better. Hence, it results in better remembrance and recalling also. Any chapter or topic that is studied in instalments puts extra pressure on the mind in recollecting as to what was studied earlier. It also takes more time and makes lesser sense in relating with the current topic. It directly results into the wastage of the limited, precious time and efforts.

Advice: Kindly read this chapter two to three times during the day, today. It helps to get some of the important methods ingrained into the subconscious mind. It is a gradual process. Hence, try to devote more time as far as possible.

***

DAY 22

How to Cope with the Pressure of Studies?

This chapter will focus on the various reasons for the ever increasing stress levels in the life of the common man. It will also analyse the negative impact it is creating in the lives of students. Once, we get to know the factors that are troubling us then it will become much easier for us to handle and tackle them. We will also look forward to the steps to be taken to avoid unpleasant situations and other remedial measures to be executed to keep ourselves relaxed so as to ensure normal functioning in our daily life.

Let us first address the issues where students find difficulty and unnecessarily get stuck up in various small problems. These are:

Time Management

All the activities and efficiency of a school is largely dependent on its time table. Similarly, result-oriented students have planned a system of studying for themselves which they

Today's Date: __ / __ / ____
(Kindly write with a Pencil)

follow strictly. These are the students who excel in their regular studies, achieve their targets as well as become meritorious. This is the only way for studying for more hours and gradually covering all the syllabus. Whenever a system is followed, the mind feels relaxed and tension-free, and it works more efficiently.

Be Organised

Your system of studying should be properly organised. The surroundings should be tidy, neat and clean. It has a direct and positive impact on the mind. The room where you study, your study table, your books, notebooks and others important tools like the pencil box, calculator, computer, stationery, etc. should all be well placed and readily available. If all these small things are not prepared well in advance then it creates unnecessary flutter in the mind. It blocks the required mental energy and resources important for studying and its remembrance thereof.

Good Environment

Another important factor is good environment. It refers to many different aspects like peace and harmony at home amongst family members; friendly terms and conditions with your neighbours, friends and relatives; love and self-respect in the society, etc. It also refers to neat, clean, tidy and hygienic surroundings which have adequate provision for light and air ventilation. All such provisions give a great positive push to the mind. In this way, the mind works faster and with more efficiency for longer duration altogether. There are also negligible signs of fatigue.

Different Methods of Learning

Each and every person has their own capacity and capabilities of studying, learning and remembrance, and has also developed their own methods in this regard over the years. Some students like to read and repeat their subjects themselves, some read it in slow pitch voice whereas some others read it reasonably louder. Yet there are some others who like to read and write simultaneously while some others like to read, learn and give oral tests to each other.

The student himself has to decide which method suits him the most. A different approach maybe required for different subjects in accordance to the availability of time, because availability of time is a very big constraint in today's highly competitive and high paced world. So, students must adopt that method which is more suitable and convenient to them.

Visualise Achievements

Students with the help of their parents and teachers should keep on meeting other students who have achieved great success in studies, competitive exams and are meritorious. They should also meet people who are highly successful in their respective careers. This will give students a fair idea of the pride and respect one gets on being successful. This kind of interactions will prompt them to think and feel the joy of being ahead of others. Gradually, they will also start to visualise such occasions of being honoured in the society.

This method is in itself a kind of self-motivation and has proved to be highly beneficial in inspiring students. Students are now found to be more disciplined towards dedicating their time and efforts seriously in achieving their goals. Motivation pushes students forward, creates self-confidence and energises them. Initially it happens at their mental level and then at the physical level to step up their efforts to keep moving towards their goals. This proves to be highly beneficial in avoiding a breakdown at the mental or physical level. This is more important at the time of preparations when there is immense pressure to excel and be meritorious.

Be Optimistic with "I CAN DO IT" Attitude

Motivation of any kind becomes short-lived and somewhat useless if the students themselves are not optimistic of their own success. The "I CAN DO IT" attitude is very important throughout life. But it has to be developed in students' life itself because during these years, students are full of energy, strength and vigour. They can put their plans into action and also take up new challenges to perform, and judge their success every now and then.

Keep Upgrading

A school is a place which trains students in numerous ways. It also provides a platform to all the students to use its resources and facilities, talents and knowledge of the academic staff. Now, it is up to the students to explore, experiment and learn new things thereof. All such achievements help students to stay ahead of others. It gives them a feeling of satisfaction and further motivates them to keep working harder and smarter in order to be more successful in life.

Adequate Rest and Sleep

Ensure yourself enough rest and sleep. Generally, it is felt that 6–8 hours of undisturbed and sound sleep is enough to relax the mind and body of a normal person. But sleeping hours can vary from person to person. So, you must relax and sleep as per your own body's requirements only and not according to what others say. But you must also keep in check that you do not oversleep and shorten your studying hours. Oversleeping makes the mind dull and lethargic. So balancing is also equally important here.

Adequate rest and sleep greatly improves the capability and power of the mind in studying for longer durations, learning and remembrance. And during examinations it helps in clear and faster recalling of things. It is also a great stress buster. Tensions and worries keep on multiplying whenever students are short on sleep. Time spent lying on the bed before the actual sleep should not be counted as part of the sleeping hours. Students should also try to be calm, relaxed and get themselves rid of all their worries so as to be able to have a sound sleep.

Relief & Avoid Stress

The most important thing for students is to study for longer durations with a relaxed and calm state of mind for quick and better remembrance. For this, they should study with short breaks in between. Otherwise, worries will overshadow and influence their daily workings in a bad and devastating manner. It will only leave them more confused and frustrated. Here are suggested some ideas which would be of great help to all the students. You may underline a part of these points for a quick referral later on.

Dos:

- Preferably, study with your room closed, if possible, with minimum distractions and noises of any kind.
- The source and direction of the light should not disturb your eyes directly. It helps to lessen fatigue caused to the eyes.
- Paper quality and printing should be good. Then the receptivity by the mind is much faster and clearer. Most preferably, the paper used for reading and writing should be white. It should also be a bit thick so that the matter written on the one side is not visible on the other side. Each and every font should be printed clearly so that it is read clearly and quickly, and not misread or misunderstood.
- Begin your studies at a time after you have fulfilled your family responsibilities so as to avoid any unnecessary longer breaks in between.
- Take a short break for 3-5 minutes only in between when suddenly you begin feeling drowsy, heaviness in the eyes, feeling bored and uninterested, or the topic starts making lesser sense or starts bouncing off the mind, etc.
- Keeping the goals in their minds, during these small breaks students must try to refresh themselves in a shortcut way. Like munch on some favourite dish of your liking, have some hot or cold beverage but the best is plain water or some fresh fruit juice or fresh vegetable juice. They may perform yoga or some stretching exercises like touching their feet or bending sideways or take a small walk in the room or in the surroundings. You may also give your hands, feet and face a refreshing wash with fresh water, etc.
- Another short and very effective method is to calmly take about 10-12 deep breaths, hold it inside for 5-10 seconds and release it slowly. At this time give a feeling to your subconscious mind that your stress, tensions, worries and fatigue are also being released along with the outgoing breath.
- In this technique, we have increased the intake of oxygen to the mind and the body, thereby improving the circulation of blood.
- Another very effective method is to laugh loudly and uncontrollably at least 10-12 times at one go along with raising your hands up.
- Initially, it may appear to be somewhat funny and embarrassing to some people. But its results are astonishing. Whenever a person is

happy and laughs loudly, the brain secretes certain hormones and there is also greater intake of oxygen which relieves the mind of its worries and fatigue.

Even though laughing is prompted artificially but the same process takes place naturally. Secondly, it also helps to clear out our lungs which enables the body to increase the intake of oxygen and release more of bad breath and odour from our bodies. Best results are felt when performed under a lush green tree in a park away from a busy road.

- A short bath energises the body and mind simultaneously. Water is composed of oxygen and it is the lifeline of the human body. So the body and mind, both greatly feel refreshed after bathing. Secondly, it cleanses the body of sweat, dirt or any other kind of bad odour. Thirdly, it opens up the pores of the body which enables it to breathe and feel fresh.
- Subjects, topics or chapters should be interchanged sometimes at regular intervals to keep students away from getting bored and worn out. Many times, studying a single subject for longer duration starts bouncing off one's mind. So it is better to switch subjects to remain active, save time from getting wasted, avoid being bored and the interest and motivation level also does not dip.

Don'ts:

- Refreshment breaks should not exceed more than five minutes at the most. Otherwise, the link with the subject matter being studied starts getting off the mind.
- Not a good time to chat with friends, neither personally nor on the phone or the internet. It can create great distraction. This break is not meant for enjoyment, but is just a small gap in between studies.
- Do not indulge in heavy exercises for longer durations, otherwise, the body will get tired and the mind may start feeling drowsy.
- Never ever think of consuming tobacco of any kind, cigarette smoking or alcohol, drugs, etc. This is a growing stage for your body and mind. It should be nourished well with good things. But all such things damage your body to a great extent which is visible only during the later years of life. Kindly avoid.
- Even drinking tea, coffee or cold drinks should be limited and in

small quantities only. These things dehydrate the body as well as decrease the flow of oxygen in the blood.

Students have to take care of the do's and don'ts themselves. Self indulgence of any kind can prove to be harmful for them. They should not force upon themselves any method only because someone else is comfortable with it. Our body and mind is a supercomputer created and gifted by God to all of us. Its sanctity should be maintained and taken care of. Then only we can expect full concentration in our studies and hence, better grades.

Take Lighter Meals

Many times, the food that we eat also makes us lethargic, drowsy and lazy. It is more so if taken in a heavy quantity or after longer durations. So, prefer lighter meals and try to have it 4 to 5 times in a day instead of the regular 2 or 3 larger ones. This type of arrangement will keep you fresh, charged-up and energised throughout the day. It also aids in better digestion, thus avoiding any kind of discomfort in the stomach or complaints of acidity or heartburns, etc.

Also prefer to have home cooked food only. It contains all the necessary ingredients for the optimum working of the physical and mental functions. Kindly avoid all kinds of fast food, junk food, sold by the street vendors or even restaurants and hotels, etc. on a regular basis. Occasionally, it is okay for a change of mood.

Also, keep in check the intake of salt and sugar. These two have adverse effects on our health if consumed in large amounts. You must have heard that 'Excess of Everything is bad'. Eating excess amounts of toffees, chocolates, sweet-meat, sugar or goods made from sugar can be harmful in all ages. Similarly, fast food, junk food and other preserved food contains salts and many types of preservatives. Excess intake of such foods can be harmful. Hence, exercise control over all these.

Light Physical Exercise for 10-15 Minutes

Physical exercise is important to regulate the body functions. It is also good for the circulation of blood in the body as well as towards the mind. Such exercises should be chosen that give movement to all parts of the body. Preferably it should be undertaken for 15-30 minutes in a day either on a daily basis or on alternate days. But it should not cause any kind of physical stress or fatigue. Otherwise the limited mental energy will get engaged towards its relaxation and it will disturb our schedule of studies.

Aerobics and swimming should also be undertaken but only once or twice a week. It may be done for at least an hour preferably on a holiday or a half working day. Both these activities are a combination of exercise as well as a great method of relaxation. Both of these are great stress busters also. Swimming in a calm and relaxed manner is also a form of meditation.

A Nap for 10-15 Minutes

A nap is a short sleep for 10-15 minutes only. It has been done to refresh and energise the body and mind in a short duration only, and without making the person feel sleepy or lazy afterwards. It should be taken just after the daytime meal when there is a sudden gush of drowsiness. A nap at this time satisfies the cycle of sleep which naturally forces the body to wink.

A nap after lunch does wonders for the body and mind. A person starts to have the same feeling of freshness that he was having in the morning itself. Now he is ready to work with the same energy and enthusiasm for the remaining part of the day. This is what we want and suggest to the students as well. There are many offices around the world where a separate room has been provided for the staff to nap. This ultimately leads to better productivity for the company and lesser stress for the staff.

Introspection

Introspection means self-analysis. It is human nature to make mistakes, but to realise and correct those mistakes depends a lot on the human beings themselves. For this introspection is a must. It can only be done when a person sits alone with his thoughts, thinks deeply over them and then truly analyses his actions in totality.

There are some other measures also which help students in concentrating on their studies in a better way.

- **Confide Your Worries in Someone Trustworthy:** Sharing and discussing your thoughts, worries, ideas and day-to-day activities with someone you trust can give a great relief. It will also give a boost to your emotional well-being and in turn, cause you lesser tensions and anxiety. This will also give you new directions and a different view-point on the concerned issues. It will further highlight the differences in thinking that were causing you unnecessary worries. In this way, you also learn and develop a mature way of thinking and adopt a more positive approach towards your life.

- **Do not Sit Idle or Remain Alone for Longer Durations:** Such situations also aggravate your problems and create unnecessary worries, confusions and discomfort in the mind. It disturbs your studies very badly. Hence, it is advisable to always spend some time with friends, go out to a nearby park, play games or even take up a social cause, etc.

  The idea is to spend some time with others thus avoiding to remain alone or sit idle. This will let you to indulge yourself in some activity, remain busy, feel happy and contented. This will in turn enable you to keep the mind engaged, fresh and full of news, ideas and thoughts.

- **Relax:** Whenever a problem or a worry pops up and starts creating sudden upheaval in the mind, then it is advisable to take some rest. It could be in the form of a quick bath or even a swim. Sleeping for some time is also recommended. Such activities provide good immediate relief and relaxation to the mind. It helps to ease the nerves and hence, the tensions to a great extent.

  When the mind is relaxed, workable solutions will appear on its own. During such situations, some people tend to smoke a cigarette or consume some wine or whisky as well. To them, it appears to relax them but in reality, it only aggravates the problem further. Moreover, it is injurious to your health and at such a time of stress intoxication confuses the mind more. This could result into wrong decisions, as well.

- **Holidaying:** For certain problems and issues which demand more time and analysis, taking a longer break would be more advisable and suitable. As per your convenience, a short trip or a picnic with family or friends can be planned for a day or two. This is a natural phenomenon which works wonders for all of us. Though it may also be good to be cut-off from your routine life for a minimum of 4-5 days. In this way, your mind will get ample time in cooling off from the existing problems. In the backdrop, your subconscious mind will analyse the situation in totality and workout probable solutions.

- **Undertake One Task at a Time:** Many times, a situation arises when tasks begin to pile up one after the other and the existing tasks in hand also start taking a back seat. In such circumstances, never lose your temper or patience and get irritated. With just some planning, along with time management, will get all the jobs accomplished very soon.

  Whenever a new assignment is handed over to you, always accept it with a positive attitude. This gives a very satisfactory message to the mind. It does not get hyperactive and keeps itself calm and composed. First go through the requirements and directions of the given work, prioritise them and then get started on it one by one. In this way, the mind will work very smoothly and all the work will get finished very soon.

- **Neglect Unimportant Issues and Gossips:** These things clutter, distract and disturb the mind badly. So it should be avoided as far as possible. Instead a more humble and mature approach should be adopted towards all such things that come your way.

- **Do Not Interfere in Others' Affairs:** This is a very common trait found in many people. They unknowingly get themselves entangled into it and create a mess in their own lives. This is a kind of chain reaction which goes on multiplying. It further develops unnecessary clutter in their minds which is hard to get rid of after some time. This is a natural phenomenon. So, do not become a mediator or a preacher and interfere in the lives of other people. Instead it would be better to focus only on your goals and the means to achieve them.

- **Talk Less and Listen More:** This is another important lesson which proves to be very useful throughout your life. First of all, it saves much of your useful energy which gets wasted in talking endlessly. Secondly, it also creates unnecessary burden on the mind. It renders the mind dull which is unable to study or learn properly after some time.

Thirdly, you share your deepest thoughts and secrets which should not have been told otherwise. Fourthly, by listening more, you give yourself a chance to learn wise thoughts and other important things from other people's knowledge and experiences. And lastly, a good listener is always given due regard and importance by everyone in the society.

God also wants us to listen more and talk less. That is why he has endowed us with two ears to listen more, and only one mouth to talk comparatively less.

- **Think Positive – Work Positive:** Every person comes across different types of good and bad events in their lives. It is a continuous process. Bad events can range from an important task from getting delayed or cancelled to the demise of a person in the immediate family. You are also one of them. The message being conveyed to you is that you must also live your daily life in a normal way whenever any mis-happening occurs. Life should not stop or come to a standstill. You must develop positivity and a good approach towards life in general. Gradually the pain and sadness will fade away.

- **Face Problems with Peace and Patience:** Any type of problem or challenge in this world can be resolved with its results favourable to us. But the person must possess two things, i.e. Peace and Patience. Any person who faces his problems with due patience, thinks and works over them peacefully, will be more courageous and tactful in gaining control over his adverse circumstances. Decisions taken out of impatience or frustration can be minimised and will never hurt him. Hence, such people are quite successful in life.

- **Do Not be Narrow-minded:** A person who is stubborn, egoistic or narrow-minded in his approach can never enjoy his life in true sense. He will miss out on even small moments of happiness coming his way despite his being successful or wealthy. It is all in the mind. Positive attitude makes a great difference in the well-being and satisfaction of even a common man. His mind also tends to remain active, healthy and happy which is important for its optimum working and better results.

> **Advice:** *Repeatedly read the points at least three to four times today. They will change your life for ever.*

***

Practice Session - III

Develop Your Imagination Power

- Create a new tune on a musical instrument for an existing favourite song.
- Try to develop a new recipe by your imagination.
- Imagine a car which may fly when the roads are covered with snow.
- Think of developing new kind of life jackets which are bigger and much lighter to save larger number of people during natural calamities.
- Think of developing other additional uses of the mobile phones, television remote control devices or using their batteries, etc.
- Think about new methods of recycling of used, torn or worn out clothes, shoes, items made of paper or wood, etc., and so on…

Methods to Improve Your Decision-Making Abilities

- Start maintaining a small notepad or a pocket diary.
- A work once mentioned on a certain date should be taken-up on that date.
- Refer your previous decisions and experiences while in taking decisions.
- First, try to understand the problem in its actual sense that is troubling you, then only work on finding its solution.

Precautions while Taking Decisions

- Never take decisions in haste or due to shortage of time.
- Never take decisions when you are being pressurised by others.
- Never take decisions without analysing each and every

Today's Date: __ / __ / ____
(Kindly write with a Pencil)

aspect of the concerned subject matter.

- Never take decisions when you are drunk, tired or feeling drowsy.

Methods to Improve Your Concentration and Focus

- Whenever you are alone, close your eyes, take a deep breath slowly and release it slowly. Repeat this 5-10 times.
- Undertake only one activity at a time whenever possible.
- Do not let your mind wander away from the task at hand.
- Always sit upright and use a stable table and chair while studying or working.
- Always wear neat and clean clothes to feel comfortable.
- Always take lighter meals.
- Try to avoid too much oily, spicy, cold or fast food.
- Regular bathing also refreshes the body and mind together.
- Use natural light for most of the time.
- Never compromise on your sleeping hours.
- Adopt and follow a simple and positive attitude towards life.

A Special Method to Improve Your Observation

Meditation

- Meditation with eyes open – Focus your eyes on a fixed object which is 2-3 metres away from you.
- Meditation with eyes closed – Sit still and straight. Now take a slow, deep breath inside. Now exhale your breath slowly. Repeat it 3-5 times. Keep sitting still, calm and idle. Just sit idle and silently. Do not try to focus on anything. There is only darkness and peace inside.
- Preferably meditate in a silent place. This is especially important in the initial days of practice. And if there happens to be some kind of noise, try to enjoy it and let it just pass through your mind. Stopping it will disturb you more. So, it is better to let it pass through you. In this way you will be able to keep yourself more relaxed and undisturbed paving the way for eternal bliss.
- Having practised the previous stage, now you have trained your mind to meditate anywhere.

Formation of Different Words

Using the letters mentioned below, create as many words as possible. You have to use all the different letters only once to form words. So, get started.

Exercise 1: R A H C E S O K T N

SEARCH REACH CARE RACE CAKE TAKE

TOKEN ... ...

Exercise 2: A P P R O P R I A T E

RATE PIRATE ATE TEAR ROPE EAR

REAR ... ...

Code Language

Code language is a method of remembering things in an easier and comfortable way. Code here means to remember things by some other name or sign.

Exercise 1: Now let us practise the code language you had learnt in the chapter. Match the words and numbers with their respective codes by drawing a line.

Numbers		Codes for Numbers
TWO		HIVE
3		EVEN
FIVE		SEEING
SIX		HEAVEN
7		LIFTING
EIGHT		TREE
10		DEN
11		NINTH INN
TWELVE		SHELVE
FIFTEEN		WEIGHT
16		WHO
NINETEEN		FIX

Exercise 2: Here you have to write the missing words or the codes.

Numbers	Codes for Numbers	Numbers	Codes for Numbers
	TREE	SEVEN	
FOUR		EIGHT	
	WHO		MINE
ONE		5	
	HURTING		EVENING
	FIX		SHELVE
TEN			SEEING
	FLOORING	FIFTEEN	
	HEFTY		HEAVEN
NINETEEN		18	

Exercise 3: Here you have to write the missing numbers for their codes, or missing codes for their numbers. After completion, check and compare it out with the respective chapter.

Numbers	Codes	Numbers	Codes	Numbers	Codes
38.	CH		CF	BD	
	BB	55.			EB
40.	DZ		BE	CG	
54.		38.		53.	EC
	BG		EA	42.	
43.		23.	BC		FA
39.	CI		44.	EF	
26.		30.	CZ		33.
	EG	FC		41.	
45.		58.	EH	34.	CD
29.	BI		47.		FZ

	EZ	FE		DI	
28.		32.	CB		35.
	CA		46.	FD	
62.	FB	EI			48.

Example 3: Relate the things of your shopping list with something. Fill in the missing connection.

SHOPPING LIST	CODE	REMINDED BY
	My Beautiful Hair (as seen every morning)	Reflection in a Car Mirror
DETERGENT	Feeling of Freshness	
TOOTHBRUSH		Dirty Teeth of the Shopkeeper
TEA	My Favourite Aroma Every Morning	
CHOCOLATE		A Child Eating Chocolate on the Way
	Sharp Pencil Tip	Broken Tip of My Pencil in the Geometry Box
MEDICINE	Lifeline of My Grandfather	
	I Cannot do without My Mobile	Low Battery Beep by the Mobile Handset

***

DAY 24

Meditation – The Key to Success

Meditation is a unique and very simple way of giving rest to the mind in the most natural way. Nowadays, meditation is the most sought after remedy being adopted by one and all. But it is also most misunderstood and misinterpreted method offered by numerous self-styled *gurus*. Kindly do not be misled by the promotions and preaching of some of these greedy people. Instead please initiate some research on your own in this regard and find out their genuinity. Also, check your suitability before joining any group of people or an organisation.

Every human being has been gifted with a unique mind, great inner strength and energy which unlocks further when he begins meditating. It will guide him naturally on the journey forward. So, start meditating as soon as possible without much delay or waiting for a *guru* or a sect. Practically, there is no need for someone's help. It is very simple and easy to practise.

Today's Date: __ / __ / ____
(Kindly write with a Pencil)

How to Meditate

Sit idle, without doing anything or thinking about anything, with your eyes closed for a few minutes everyday, preferably after a bath, swim or a workout. The body and mind become fresh and are in a natural rhythm with each other after a good bath. You may either sit on chair, on the floor with your legs crossed over or by standing still. Remember that your backbone should always be straight in any position you happen to meditate.

The whole body should not be tensed but in a relaxed state with the right posture. In the earlier days of practising and learning meditation, introspection happens on its own. It is a natural phenomenon. Meditation is more effective when carried out in isolation without any noise or activity in the vicinity. Though there are other methods of meditation also, but this is the most effective, less time consuming and the results are far more productive and lifelong.

Meditation and Introspection are interrelated to each other. Introspection means analysis of one's own thoughts and actions with oneself in the mind on the subconscious level. When meditation is done on a daily basis introspection happens for the first few minutes only. Saving of useful things and deletion of discarded information happens automatically. That is the magic of our mind.

When the mind becomes clear of its thoughts and worries, it paves the way for a smooth and direct journey into the unknown. This is where deep meditation begins on its own. It is a natural phenomenon. Just keep sitting idle, without wandering and doing nothing at all. Just keep flowing and drifting away with the flow. Relax and enjoy each and every moment of this newly found bliss. This is the only way of reaching here. It cannot be initiated directly without getting rid of clutter, thoughts, ideas, worries or tensions from the mind.

Meditation is a way of directing the mind on the subconscious level to gradually slow down its working processes related with our mind. By this way, we provide our minds some time to take rest and relaxation. If we can meditate everyday, we can unload unimportant things from our minds on a daily basis. Though the actual duration of relaxation may vary from a few seconds to a few minutes only but still it makes a great difference. It helps in relieving numerous thoughts and worries that were blocking the mental energies to let the mind work more smoothly and efficiently.

If you start practising meditation on a daily basis, you will soon feel the positive differences taking place in your life. It could be regarding your clarity in thinking, studying and learning new things. It will also greatly help in remembering and recalling information, analysing and tackling with problems, interpersonal skills and relationships, etc.

There is another method of meditation which is also suggested to people. In this method, you are supposed to focus on a thing with your eyes wide open. All those people who are not able to meditate with their eyes closed, are suggested this method to start meditating with their eyes open.

Here, people are directed to focus on a specific object. It could be either a flame of a burning candle or a black dot on the wall. Both of these should be kept at a distance of 2-3 metres which are clearly visible to the eyes. There should not be any movement or noise of any kind nearby so that a proper focus can be formed. With a little practice, it becomes easy.

The main idea here is to stop engaging yourself in all other activities, sit still in a specific position and focus on an object. This method appears to be effective but here the mind is still working. Secondly, decluttering of the mind has not taken place. Initially it seems to be working. But gradually people start losing interest as it does not show them positive results even after many days. This is quite natural. Whenever you start noticing positive results from an activity, your mind will be more inclined and motivated in pursuing it further.

There are four steps to complete the meditation process:

First, is to cut the connection of the mind from the daily routine life and activities for a few minutes.

Second, is to declutter and get the mind rid from the discarded things which further unlocks the mental energies from getting wasted.

Third, is to relax the mind and direct the renewed mental energies towards the more useful pursuits.

Fourth, is to gradually cleanse, activate and energise all the seven *chakras*, the energy centres, of the body.

In this way, the rhythm of both the body and mind start working in totality and synchronization. This further helps to repair the various mental and physical problems developed over the years. Neurological problems are found to be the most beneficial whose results can be noticed within a few days only.

Since meditation is not any kind of a religious activity or a ritual, hence there are no rules or regulations. But there are some simple precautions only so that its experience and feelings can be felt in a more positive way. These are:

- Consult your doctor if you are suffering from any physical ailment. Also, if you start feeling any kind of discomfort in sitting or standing in a position for a longer duration. But, remember that your backbone has to be straight during meditation.
- Interact with a few people who have been meditating for quite some time. You will get to know its benefits, the insights that you would develop and other avenues that could possibly open up.
- Meditation should be done at a Comfortable Place: There should be no foul smell of any kind, shouldn't be too hot, too cold, unbearable humidity or moisture, should not be too brightly lit or damp dark, etc. In a nutshell, the place chosen for meditation can be a room suitable and comfortable to you. Or even some place outside in a park, nearby a lake, river or a waterfall but without any noise or other distractions.
- Avoid Mediation During Discomfort: Proper rest should be given whenever there arises an illness, any other discomfort or when the body and mind are extremely tired. A break in such situations proves to be beneficial in the long run.

> **Advice:** *Meditation is the key to success and happy life. So learn to meditate with complete concentration.*

DAY 25

Preparation of Notes

Notes are the summarised version of the whole chapters, other important and miscellaneous topics, etc. It also contains the crux of the subject matter in a short form. Notes are prepared so that the revisions and the preparations become easier during the examination days. Time is crucial and limited in those days. Notes help to save and make good use of the limited time. In the days of exams, it is not possible to go through the whole syllabus.

At this time only the chosen material, the notes, that had been extracted from the syllabus should be referred to. It also puts lesser load on the mind. The mind is already under extreme pressure and anxiety due to performance and outcome of results. Hence, notes are extremely important, and play a crucial role in good learning and remembrance. This in turn results into faster recalling of information, higher speed in writing, better grades in the exams and increased chances of being meritorious.

Preparing Notes

- Always use a sharp-edged pencil so that the writing can be correct and easily read thereafter, and any mistake in writing or alterations can be made by simply erasing and writing again. Anything written on a clear white colour paper has a very good bearing on the mind. Learning becomes much faster. Hence, paper of rough quality or the coloured one should be avoided. Notes prepared by using pens and cuttings thereof have a very adverse effect on the learning process.
- Your mind should be fresh and free from all external thoughts that are not related to your studies. This will ensure faster and better learning with good recalling later on whenever required.
- First of all, read the whole chapter slowly and steadily, understand it line by line, repeat it twice or thrice as per the difficulty

Today's Date: __ / __ / ____
(Kindly write with a Pencil)

felt. By now you must have understood the crux of the topic. Now, start reading the chapter again from the beginning and keeping the crux in mind start noting down the important points one by one.

- Notes should be written down in form of points. Points are more easily readable just by a quick glance over them. Learning is rather slow and takes a longer time when notes are prepared in the form of a paragraph. It is also more confusing when read hurriedly.
- If the points are given some titles also, either in bold or by way of an underline, they could turn out to be more effective and useful.
- Notes should be prepared in such a way which is easily understandable by oneself. Later on during the preparation and exam days this easy format helps a lot in revising the syllabus in a very short time.
- You can also underline or highlight important points in your textbooks itself. Small important noting can also be mentioned besides the marked portions. Preferably do the underlining with a light pencil only as it is least disturbing to the mind.
- Where the whole paragraph is important, make a small marking besides it. This helps to maintain the cleanliness of the book. It is also much easier for the mind to repeat it with the same comfort again.
- Books and other study material that is borrowed from the library, friends or other sources should never be marked in any way. Instead make a photostate copy of the important pages and then make notes according to your suitability.
- There is very common practice among students in borrowing, exchanging and copying notes from each other. This is not the right method of studying. Because in this way you pass the exams without understanding your syllabus in its true sense and meaning. This system will never help you in scoring good grades, being meritorious or in building a successful and bright career for yourself.
- Quotable quotes, definitions or examples mentioned by various learned people should be read, understood and learned in the same way they are mentioned. Shortening them or converting them into notes will end its actual sense, value and true meaning for the purpose it was quoted.

- Prepare your notes with full enthusiasm and motivation. Reading and writing the crux of the topic with its deep study and understanding enables good learning at the writing stage itself. The mind is very active at this time. Then revising those notes ensures better learning.

Advice: Prepare your notes properly to be meritorious.

***

DAY 26

Time Management

Time Management refers to the fine balance that has to be maintained between the ratio of 'Time Utilised' to 'Time Wasted'. All those people who *utilise their time* more than wasting it tend to be more successful in their lives, whereas people who *waste their time* more than utilising it in useful pursuits are found to be repenting all their lives. Time Management is the most challenging aspect of today's high paced modern society. Whosoever learns to manage and utilise his time well can achieve his targets, be meritorious, successful, enjoy his life and be happy for ever. This is one of the major areas which makes the difference between success and failure in life. Here a person proves to be an asset for himself, his organisation as well as for his nation. He is also able to grab high positions and the most sought after designations where he is responsible for undertaking and executing important assignments and projects with his skills, knowledge and wisdom.

You must have come across the phrase that 'Everybody has 24 hours in a Day'. But do you know what does this actually mean? Also, kindly do not feel afraid or get bogged down when you hear the term 'Time Management'. We must always study the basics first of any given topic to understand it and evaluate the importance it has in our lives. Then it will be easier for us to follow it and benefit from it.

The 24-hours phrase does not make much sense but rather confuses a person more. It creates fear and tension in his mind. He gets a feeling that he is wasting his entire 24 hours in a day and he starts getting stressed

Today's Date: __ / __ / ____
(Kindly write with a Pencil)

in whatever he does and fails miserably again and again. This happens because the quality time left over with any person is just a few hours in a day which can actually be used or wasted. The rest of the time gets used in daily routine activities like sleeping, going to the school or office and other mundane activities during the day.

Now, we have come across two categories and time management has to be implemented effectively in both of these to get good results. First, is the optimum utilisation and saving of time required for carrying out the routine activities, and second, is to set a time table for the remaining quality time. Your attitude and habits play an important role in managing your limited time and resources. This will differentiate you from the rest of the crowd. Let us analyse the basic difference.

Studying with an Open & Positive Attitude: In this way, you remain active in whatever you do during the day – be it in the school, at home or even while travelling. Everything that you observe is a part of the learning process and can aid you in your future. And by remaining alert you can keep a vigil on the events happening around you. You will also keep on looking out for ways to somehow save your time in whatever you do.

Other people also recognise and extend support or opportunities to those people only who are sincere, honest and hard working in their approach. Being alert and active you are likely to come across plenty of opportunities in your life and would also able to grab the right one at the right time.

Studying with a Closed & Negative Attitude: With such an approach, many people remain inactive, lazy and casual in their approach in whatever they do. Being alert or maintaining an active life is neither a part of their thinking nor a part of their life. They rather like to keep their life dull and easy going, thereby missing out on many opportunities coming their way. Such people also miss out on the ways of saving their valuable time and let it get wasted in routine activities. These are the people who blame their luck and God afterwards.

"Your Attitude Determines Your Altitude in Life."

The following points will guide you through various steps as to how effectively you can plan and manage your time. These are:

- First of all, after reading this chapter, do not make immediate or drastic changes to your way of living and studying. Rather be slow and steady in your approach.
- For being meritorious, you should always study as if you are

preparing for an exam to be held the very next day. You should be concerned with your books and studies only.

- Kindly arrange a room or a small apartment having the basic amenities. You would not be disturbed by the daily chores and other disturbances taking place in the house.
- As shown at the end of this chapter, make a chart on a chart paper of all the activities, that you are involved with throughout the day starting from Monday to Sunday. Lay out the chart paper in landscape form and fill the boxes with a pencil so that it could be altered easily. Note that the ideas mentioned here are only an example and not suggestions. Kindly prepare it according to your own suitability. It should be ideal and provide enough time for sleeping, eating, playing, relaxing besides studying.
- Now, also prepare a similar weekly report and fill it with a pencil each night before going to sleep. Please no cheating here. It is for your own good and you are not supposed to share it with others, not even with your best friends. Evaluate it yourself, find where you have progressed, where you are still lacking and can make further improvements. You may take the advice of your mentors in helping you with re-scheduling your systems.
- Keep in regular touch with class toppers, intellectuals and other successful people in your neighbourhood. Such meetings and interactions will keep you motivated to cut down on wasting your precious time and studying more instead. Without enough inspiration and motivation, preparing and filling-up such time-tables are not at all enough in this direction.
- The importance of time and its proper utilisation should be taught since early childhood so that with the passage of time your children can themselves realise its necessity and importance. Under your guidance, they will also learn to plan it effectively. They can thus improve upon themselves by the time they reach higher classes. Self-realisation is more inspiring and result-oriented than constant nagging and punishments.
- Your studying pattern should be such that it always keeps you ahead of the class. Always maintain flexibility in your time table. This will help you to adjust any emergency or responsibility at any time without disturbing your regular studies. Provisioning done in this way is very helpful in being meritorious. Later on it adds extra hours in preparations also.

- A school is an educational institution but it provides many other benefits and opportunities also. Participate in all the activities carried out in the school whole heartedly. Do your best and always try to achieve a good position. School days will never come again in your life. Presence of mind, motivation, courage and energy is the best during these years. Make its optimum use. It helps to shape up your future in the best possible way.
- For overall success and achievements in life, never ever become a bookworm. Being studious and hard working is good but other activities also carry equal weightage and importance. Do spend enough time with all types of your friends but, in the school only. It also helps you to unwind from your routine of daily studies. You would feel energised when you return home from the school. This will further help you to save your precious time at home which could have otherwise got wasted in entertaining or refreshing yourself. Once home, follow your time table seriously with an upbeat mood and without any laziness. Always keep your priorities and goals in mind.
- Friendship and networking done in the school now will prove to be very helpful throughout your life. Here you get an opportunity to befriend all types of students belonging to different and varied backgrounds. This is quite helpful, especially at managerial positions, marketing jobs or in liaison fields. You get to know the different traits and habits of people and how to deal with them efficiently. It also greatly helps in establishing and maintaining connections later in life.
- Many times, studying a certain subject according to your mood results into better understanding and learning. So, the pattern of studying may vary from the time table already laid out. There is no problem as such. The only idea here is to study for more hours with the best utilisation of time without pressurising the mind. It results into good learning and remembrance.
- Here it is advisable to take up the difficult topics first and gradually shift to lighter and easy subjects later on. In this way, taking up easier subjects later on will not exert much pressure on the mind which is now feeling a bit tired. So, this approach enables continuity in studying without longer breaks in between and thus, saving time as well.
- Always adopt an enthusiastic and optimistic approach towards all

the activities that you undertake. Most importantly, it will check any kind of worries and tensions entering your mind and thus, disturbing you. Any problem or negativity should be dealt with immediately so as to continue with regular studies.

- Try to delegate some of your responsibilities which you feel others can also share. This will help you to lessen your burden and save a lot of your precious time and energy.
- With regular practice and increased confidence level, now comes the time for increasing your speed in studying. This results in increasing the capacity of the mind thereby allowing it to store more things in lesser time. It also enables better learning, remembering and recalling of the stored information. Thus, all the above helps in saving time.

Besides the above mentioned tips, also remember the following:

- **Take Frequent but Small Breaks in Between** for a quick bath, drinking water, to have refreshments or to relieve yourself. This allows certain movements to your body and thus, to your limbs which had got tired while sitting in a certain position for a long duration.
- **Correct Posture** plays a very important role in the learning process. It keeps the mind alert and active which keeps you interested in your studies.
- **A Table Lamp** lightens up the table area only where the student is sitting with his books. It helps in better concentration and stops the mind in drifting away from the books. Because rest of the room is comparatively dark and damp.
- **An Alarm Clock** is a student's best friend throughout his/her life. It not only reminds him of his timings but also wakes him up on his pre-fixed time. It can also be used as a timer and have the alarm set, to alert him so that he can take up his next assignment.

Here, you have studied about managing your time effectively. You also came across many other methods which are indirectly helpful in saving time and also beneficial in many other ways.

Advice: Kindly read this chapter two to three times today. Then only it will make more sense for you.

***

Sample Time-Table

Timings	Monday	Tuesday	Wednesday	Thursday	Friday	Saturday	Sunday	Noting
5-6 am	(a) Wake-up with an Alarm, Freshen-up & Sit to Study						(m) Wake up, Go … *	
6-7 am	(b) Study & Get Ready for School							
7-8 am	(c) Get Ready & Leave for School							
8-9 am	(d) In the School	(d) In the School	(d) In the School	(d) In the School	(d) In the School	(d) In the School	(n) Back … *	
9-10 am								
10-11am							(o) Study or Go to … *	
11-12pm								
12-1 pm							(p) *	
1-2 pm								
2-3 pm	(e) Reach Home and Unwind Yourself							
3-4 pm	(f) Relax, Eat a Light Lunch and Take a Nap (15-30 Minutes only)							
4-5 pm	(g) Start Your Studies / Attend Coaching Class							
5-6 pm								
6-7 pm	(h) Have a Bath, Light Refreshments/ Snacks, Start Your Studies							
7-8 pm	(i) Studying in Your Study Room							
8-9 pm								
9-10 pm	(j) Chat & Have Dinner with Family, Take ½ Hour Break							
10-11pm	(k) Studying in Your Study Room							

11-12pm	(l) Sleeping	
12-1 am		
1-2 am		
2-3 am		
3-4 am		
4-5 am		

5-8 am -- (m) Wake-up as usual, go to park, warm up your body, exercise and play.

OR simply keep sleeping to unwind for the past week.

8-10 am -- (n) Back Home, relax, bathe, have breakfast, sit and interact with parents and family.

10-12 am -- (o) Optional, either go to sleep for some time after the physical activities in the morning, or take up studying if feeling refreshed.

12-11 pm -- (p) Visit a friend or a relative, watch a movie at home or Cineplex, lunch or dinner at a new food joint or restaurant, etc.

> **Advice:** *Sunday is the only day which we can truly spend on ourselves. Hence, devote maximum time in studying, revising all what has been taught during the past week, and self-studying for the coming week.*

Sunday is only one day between two big working weeks. Hence, use it well for yourself and stay ahead of others.

On a Single Holiday: This is the day of beating others and staying ahead of them. Because most of them would waste their time in relaxing or other leisure activities. It greatly depends on what you want from your life.

On this day, you can alter your studying and sleeping pattern to some extent. The timings may vary from the time table but you should never lessen your sleeping hours.

More Than One Holiday: Since you are more inclined and disciplined towards your studies, use the bunch of holidays to unwind as well. The purpose is to unwind only and not to waste time for enjoying. Student life is meant for studying only. *Remember, that this time will never come in your life again. Hence, use it the most now.*

DAY 27

Develop Interest in Studies

Studying for longer durations with due interest and motivation is another key to success. Some students are found to be alert and active in their studies from the very beginning. They take due interest in their studies and participate in all the activities being carried out in the school. Besides regular studies, there are co-curricular activities like sport and games, exhibitions, debates, dramas, song or dance competitions, etc. There are some other students who are somewhat slow and lazy in their approach. They are often found to be lost in day-dreaming, wandering uselessly in the school premises as well as outside after the school hours.

There are many factors which influence students in adopting a dedicated and hard working approach towards their studies. It enables them in becoming meritorious in their exams and competitions. Socio-economic background of students and psychological understanding of their parents with regard to studies are the major differentiating factors

Today's Date: __ / __ / ____
(Kindly write with a Pencil)

found amongst students. Other general factors are with regard to their upbringing and atmosphere in the family, worries and tensions in the family, mutual relationships of the parents, financial and emotional support to the students, etc.

The way of upbringing and inspiration, values and fundamentals taught to children since early ages by their parents, elders and teachers play another key role in their success. This is how they adopt a positive and a respecting attitude towards their parents, their families, their teachers and their society. And they also start to value the importance of their education, hard work, discipline, honesty and success in life.

Learning is a slow and continuous process. Sound knowledge can be gained when it is studied, understood, learnt and remembered in small parts everyday. Hence, studying and learning during exam days without understanding much is in fact deceit yourself only. Many students even pass the exams with good marks also. But even in all such achievements the proper understanding of the subject matter has not taken place.

Studying for a few days only just before the examination is also very injurious to health. Students go through intense mental and physical pressure during these days. It badly affects their nervous and digestive systems. Nervousness, confusion, headache, migraine, irritation, weariness in the eyes, examination fever, indigestion, acidity, ulcers, etc. are some of the common problems faced by the students. Some of the problems persist even after the exams and may also continue for the rest of their lives. So, not paying attention to studies from the very beginning can lead to a devastating and ruined future, both in terms of career as well as health aspects.

Moreover, the time once lost is lost forever. Once a class is passed, you cannot go back, restart and relearn. You have to move ahead only with whatever you have gained in the previous classes. And in the next upper class, you will find yourself in a more pitiable situation. It will now become more difficult for you to understand and learn the advanced topics and chapters. Previously, you had missed out on learning the techniques, methodologies and ideas behind problem solving and their solutions. So, the emphasis should be more on learning your syllabus properly besides on scoring maximum marks and achieving higher grades.

Studying from the very beginning enables students to go through the same topics several times before attempting them in the exams. It exerts negligible pressure during the preparation days. Secondly, the succeeding chapters are based on the previous ones. Hence, they make more sense and result into better understanding as well as better performance in the exams.

All the subjects are revised with a cool and relaxed state of mind during the whole year. Now, you can easily visualise your success and train your mind to feel confident about it. This technique of positive attitude is called 'Latent Learning'. In this way, your mind becomes alert and active and never feels any kind of fatigue which further enables it to give optimum performance throughout your life.

During the 20th century only, there has been an outburst of inventions, researches and discoveries in every field of human existence. Its number has far exceeded all the previous inventions and it is also increasing rapidly with each passing day. For students, it means that they now have to devote extra time and efforts in their studies as compared to students some years back because they have to learn an increased number of inventions, discoveries and their techniques applicable till date. But, since the time is limited with everyone, hence, the speed for reading, writing and understanding will have to be increased tremendously.

Every student has their own capacity of reading, writing and learning. 'Rapid Reading' can give excellent results only when the mind is relaxed, and fresh to absorb new information. Otherwise, it would result into a mere simple reading without any analysis or grasping by the mind. To keep pace with the fast running world you will have to train your mind for reading and writing at an increased pace. For this, you will have to devote 10-15 minutes on every Saturday evening and gauge your speed of reading and writing. Maintain a record also for future reference.

How to Check Your Speed

- Now with the help of a stopwatch or an alarm clock, start reading some sentences of a definite language for five minutes non-stop. The language should be the one on which your syllabus is based.
- Stop exactly after five minutes.
- Now count the number of words you read, and divide it by 5, i.e., the number of minutes the text was read.
- In this way, you will get your speed, i.e., the average number of words read per minute.
- Adopt the same method for writing and typing also.
- Repeat this exercise every Saturday evening, and observe your progress.

How to Increase Your Speed

- Beginning from Monday, take up any two subjects daily.
- Read the intended topic at a greater speed than your usual speed of reading. This will be done as a practice to increase your speed.
- After finishing reading rapidly, now repeat the same topic at your normal speed to understand it properly and proceed with your normal studies.
- Gradually, the mind will get trained to read and understand the subjects faster. Hence, the need for repeating the same text afterwards will soon diminish and finish.
- And day by day, the whole syllabus of various subjects will also get learnt and remembered by the brain at a faster speed, thus enabling it to read and cover more topics.
- This will help you to save time by studying the same syllabus in lesser time and devote the saved time towards other important projects and research work.
- Also, prepare notes of all the subjects. This is also a great time saver.
- These methods will easily lead you ahead of others.
- You will now excel in each and every subject and be meritorious.

Precautions while Rapid Reading

- Do not skip or misread words while doing rapid reading. Otherwise this will lessen your learning and increase your mistakes in spellings, grammar, tenses, punctuation as well as in the general understanding of the subject matter.

- Many times such mistakes cause blunders and awkward situations in life, raising questions about the education, learning and abilities of the person concerned.
- So, while reading, always take care to read each and every word cautiously with the right meaning and in the appropriate sense.
- While writing also, formation of the words and sentences should be complete, thus making appropriate sense and logic.
- Nowadays it has been found that vowels (a,e,i,o,u) are skipped from the words to save time. But, in fact, it confuses the mind more. Here is a small example.

Correct Way: 'Early to bed, early to rise, makes a man healthy, wealthy and wise.'

Shortcut/ Incorrect Way: 'erly t bd erly t rse mks a mn hlthy wlthy nd ws.'

- Gradually, after some years, your mind will become so confused that it may stop differentiating between the right and the wrong.

Rapid reading also alerts and sharpens the mind. Students become more active and aware in their daily routine activities also. Training of the mind should never be done according to any statistics available. But, it is more important to make a slow and steady start to it as per the current capacity of your own mind. The learning process will get better in this way only. Otherwise, the mind will again feel pressurised and tensions will surface.

Advice: *Kindly read the whole chapter at least two to three times today with special emphasis on the increasing of your speed.*

Thinking Positive & Self-Confidence

Self-confidence is another important key to success. It is also one of the major bases of a person's existence and self-respect in the society. Below mentioned are some of the phrases commonly used by people who have become extremely successful in their studies, their careers and their relationships.

To become successful, you must always adopt a positive attitude and keep saying the following phrases repeatedly several times in a day. Repetition could be either loudly, slowly or quietly in the subconscious mind. It is a very successful technique used worldwide to train the mind. It harnesses the mental energies in a specific direction and also helps to keep anxiety away.

√ Yes, I Can Do It

√ Yes, I Can Win the Race

Today's Date: __ / __ / ____
(Kindly write with a Pencil)

- √ Yes, I Can Achieve My Goals
- √ Yes, I Can Succeed
- √ Yes, I Can Pass With Good Marks
- √ Yes, I Can Stand First in the Class
- √ Yes, I Can Get This Job
- √ Yes, I Can Defeat the Enemy
- √ Yes, I Can Save My Country
- √ Yes, I Can Invent a New Medicine
- √ Yes, I Can … … … … and so on.

To develop a positive attitude, you must lead an honest and truthful life as well. For doing so, you must say the following words to yourself. A few examples are:

- √ I Love God & He also Loves Me
- √ I Believe in God & His Actions
- √ I Will Always Speak the Truth
- √ I Will Never Lie from Today
- √ I Will Never Get Angry from Today
- √ I Will Never Get Jealous from Today
- √ I Will Always Work Honestly
- √ I Will Attend My School Regularly
- √ I Will Reach Office on Time
- √ I Will Not Waste Food
- √ I Will Finish My Meals
- √ I Will Respect All Elders
- √ I Will Respect My Neighbours
- √ I Will Love Children
- √ I Will Always Follow Rules & Regulations
- √ I Will Never Harm Birds & Animals
- √ I Will Never Harm Flowers, Plants & Trees
- √ I Will Never Litter on Streets
- √ I Will Never Hurt others
- √ I Will Never … … … … … and so on.

Read the above sections loudly three times every morning before leaving for school or office, and three times before going to sleep and start observing the positive difference taking place in your life very soon.

Important Tips to Increase Your Self-Confidence:

- First of all, shortlist and note down all your fears and weaknesses. Then only you can work-out and take appropriate steps to tackle them.
- Think Positive, Act Positive and Keep Smiling. This will greatly enhance your personality. Gradually, you will begin meeting new people with the same positive attitude. With increased good energy flowing all around, your self-confidence is bound to increase on its own.
- Always remain active and alert in your activities. Gradually, you will start feeling a gush of self-confidence increasing inside you.
- Keep yourself updated with the latest happenings, especially which is directly connected with your studies. It could be through the internet, newspapers, different TV channels or maybe through friends and seniors.
- All wise, learned and successful people are generally self-confident. They always talk very politely, patiently and are good listeners. Start developing such good habits slowly and steadily.
- Increase your capabilities, though slowly by taking small steps in the beginning so that you can yourself analyse and evaluate your progress. In this way, you will also be able to initiate corrective measures immediately, and avoid any kind of displeasure or discouragement later.
- Brisk walking, moderate exercising or aerobics on alternate days or weekends will help you to keep yourself physically and mentally fit. You may choose between the morning and evening timings as per your convenience.
- Develop good and friendly contacts with people who are already successful and well respected in the society. Appreciate their hard work, dedication and success wholeheartedly. These are generally nice and humble people. They will guide you and provide all the necessary help to achieve your goals.
- Pending works confuse the mind and reduce a lot of self-confidence. Kindly avoid all delays in your works and try to finish them as soon as possible.

- Always keep yourself engaged in something or the other. Never ever sit idle or waste your time, efforts and resources in useless activities. All the time that is used constructively encourages and motivates you. Indirectly and gradually, it further increases your courage and self-confidence.

- Being good at work is one of the important ingredients of your self-confidence. For this, always keep in mind and give due consideration to all the points, big and small, in any given assignment.
- Keep your focus more on self-improvement and developing your abilities instead of getting entangled in problems, worries or tensions coming your way.
- Set your goals and targets, somewhat smaller and medium, according to your own capabilities which should seem to be achievable. They should not be according to other people's plans and goals or compete with them in any way.

Be YOURSELF always. You are better than hundreds and thousands of people out there. Each and every person is born unique and has certain qualities of their own which are quite different from others. So, stop comparing yourself with others to avoid developing any kind of inferiority complex. Instead, focus on your strengths and talents, and start improving your weaknesses. Soon, you would be at par with the most talented, successful and confident people in this world.

Advice: *This is a wonderful chapter which provides you with some of the unique and hidden secrets of the successful people. The more you repeat and practise, the better results can be expected and achieved.*

DAY 29

Days of Preparation before Examination

Preparation Days are the last few days just before the examinations. These are the utmost important days for achieving your goals, being meritorious and setting the base for your success in life. Following are the steps which will guide you as to how to spend these few important days which will shape up your future forever.

Be Fresh and Healthy

A fresh and relaxed state of mind has the capacity to store abundant information, and most importantly, in this state the retaining and retrieval power improve considerably. It means that the grasping and learning is fast and whenever you try to recall or express something, you will not get stuck or require much time in recollecting that information. This ultimately results into good speed during the exams. It increases your confidence level and you further feel motivated to perform better and excel at any cost.

Today's Date: __ / __ / ____
(Kindly write with a Pencil)

To achieve the above results, both the body and mind should be healthy. *A healthy body depends upon some light exercises and proper nourishment through a balanced diet.* It should preferably be light home cooked food, avoiding junk food and overeating. Also, ensure adequate rest, short breaks and sleeping at proper timings. Adopting of good habits and refraining from the bad ones would be an added advantage.

Students should be given:

- A healthy and light breakfast in the morning comprising hot milk with butter toast or chapati. An egg at least once or twice a week, 5-7 peeled almonds everyday which had been soaked in water overnight. It provides children with the sufficient amount of energy required during the day without any laziness.
- Consult and hire a dietician on a regular and paid basis according to your convenience and affordability. You will always be thankful to yourself for this decision. In this way you will always be under their supervision. They will prepare a diet chart suitable for you as per your own specific health and body requirements. A good diet chart would ensure good healthy and active living, avoid lethargy and illnesses.
- Although you may come across several other diet charts and tips free of cost but they may not be useful in the long run. Health and diet of every person is different from others. Such charts are not prepared keeping your specific needs in mind. Hence, they are not much useful but instead they may cause you harm. Like a teacher takes care of your education, similarly a dietician takes care of your health. Always hire a paid trainer to get ahead in life. You live only once. Hence, live well and enjoy.
- Also avoid the use of medicines, tonics, health and food supplements, etc. on your own. They should strictly be used under the supervision of a good doctor or a dietician only. Many times such things seem to be very useful in increasing memory power or remaining alert and active. But many people end up facing several negative consequences later on. Kindly be informed and avoid such things during student life.
- Students should keep themselves refreshed by taking light beverages, fresh fruit or vegetable juices, soups or seasonal fruits in between their breaks.

- During lunch, they should be given proper home-cooked food comprising *chapati, pulses, vegetables*, some *rice, curd, salad*, etc. with some sweets in the end. It creates good mood for many.
- Towards the evening, some hot milk with 4-6 biscuits should be, provided. A small portion of dry fruits at least twice a week would ensure intake of the required multi-vitamins and minerals.
- At late evenings, students should be given a light dinner so that they do not feel sleepy afterwards while studying at night. The dinner should preferably be given at least 2-3 hours before sleep. It will ensure good digestion and avoid the basic troubles of gas and acidity found with many.
- And finally, ½ - 1 glass of milk before sleep would ensure enough energy till morning and also result into good sound sleep.

A healthy mind is cultivated through a positive attitude towards life. It helps to keep stress, tensions, worries or fears as low as possible. The idea here is to keep the mind healthy and active throughout the day so that the learning is faster and better.

Motivation

Motivation gives students the push to excel in the class, be meritorious, to achieve targets, to fulfil the desires and wishes of parents. This maintains their interest in studies continuously for hours day and night.

Patience

Patience helps to keep the mind relaxed and controlled when dealing with a situation. During these days the stress of preparation is quite high which results into frequent irritations and short temperament. Only patience helps to overcome such disturbances.

Keep Away from Electromagnetic Radiation (EMR)

When electricity is passed through an electronic device containing magnets, Electromagnetic Radiation (EMR) gets released from that device. Nowadays, our lives are gradually shifting towards the use of more and more automatic and electronic devices all of which contain magnets. Some of the commonly used devices are – mobile phones, laptops and desktop computers, television, radio, refrigerator, microwave ovens, electric chimneys, washing machines, air conditioners and many other such devices. Some emit lesser radiations, while others emit more radiations. It also depends on the distance that is being maintained while using it and moreover, how frequently they are being used.

Mobile phones, radio, TV, laptop with internet are devices which receive radio frequencies also and should not be kept or held very close to the body. These frequencies combined with the electromagnetic radiation have a devastating effect on the nervous system of the body, to the brain. The use of mobile phones and laptops are the most common amongst youngsters these days and its usage is also increasing alarmingly. Kindly keep in check to use them in limits only.

Spend Most of Your Time in Your Study Room

The more one studies, the easier and more understanding of the subjects become. The mind which has been kept busy in studies will not be able to wander and hence, return to books only. It forms a kind of rotation which comes back on its own. Benefits of studying continuously are numerous and astonishing. The more children study, the more cultivated, active and sharper mind they develop.

Undertake Light Exercises in Your Room

Do some light stretching exercises in your study room, the balcony or on the terrace to freshen up yourself. Some of these could be – with your hands straight up bending your body forward, backwards or sideways. Lying down straight on a hard surface for a few minutes is also very relaxing, since most of the time the body remains in sitting position only. These exercises relax the muscles and the nerves, relieve stress and do not tire the body or mind in any way. Undertake only on an empty stomach or 3-4 hours after having your meals. You may consult a medical practitioner as well.

Body Massage

Body massage at regular intervals can be very invigorating and refreshing during these days. It relaxes both the mind and body. This is another activity which does not use your energy during the entire process. Instead it prepares you for your exams with full zeal and increased energy. If short on time, you may undertake a face and head massage only. It is also similarly refreshing.

How to Develop Interest in Difficult Subjects?

The subjects and topics of lesser interest need to be devoted more time, patience and understanding. Gradually, the subjects will start making sense and their understanding will also start improving. Such subjects should be taken up and revised along with the subjects whose exams are scheduled to be held before. Seek the help and guidance of your parents, teachers, mentors and seniors also in this aspect.

Planning

Studying with great efforts and devoting several hours, but without proper planning does not bear the desired results. All those students who study in a systematic way, maintain a regular touch with their teachers and seek their guidance from time to time have totally different results. Planning in the preparation days will be different from the planning followed throughout the year.

Study for Longer Durations

Students who study more, learn more and they also retain more. Studying for longer durations has two major benefits. The more students will read and write repeatedly the more clarity they will form in their mind and the better they will score than others. Though resting, enjoying and playing is also important, during the preparation days these activities should be curtailed.

Prefer Mornings

Studying during the early morning hours is much better and naturally charismatic for learning and retaining information. Human body has been designed by nature to work more proficiently according to the formation of day and night. Studying late during the night hours has many adverse effects also. Hence, choose and plan your own system of studying as per your own convenience.

Study in Silence

Studying in silence is a kind of studying in isolation, i.e. meditation with the books. It also saves a lot of energy. During the preparation days students should study in silence because the pressure of studies is also immense. Hence, silence will aid in better and faster learning.

Avoid Laziness

Laziness is a curse for students during their student life. It also destroys all the good qualities and good habits that students possess, and it can also prove to be highly devastating during these few preparation days.

Sit Straight

Always sit straight preferably using a table and a chair for studying. This is the most suitable position for studying with greater concentration, better learning and lesser fatigue for longer durations.

Revise and Practise Your Notes

Notes are the summary and the crux of the subject matter keeping in view that its importance is retained. It also helps to exert lesser pressure during the preparation days. With the help of notes, students are able to revise their syllabus in comparatively shorter duration. This saves a lot of their time and efforts.

Help-Guides

Help-guides are available for all subjects compiled by various professionals, teachers, lecturers and professors, academicians, etc. of their respective fields. Help guides provide another way of understanding the course material in an easy way. Some of them even have notes compiled by them, solved question papers of previous years, general test exercises, etc. These should certainly be referred but for the purpose of understanding only and not as a shortcut to copying notes.

> **Advice:** *This chapter is immensely important for students. If you keep in mind and work according to the methods suggested, you will definitely get ahead of others. It is possible that you might be knowing some of the techniques, but following them will bear you results. Hence, adopt them from today itself.*

DAY 30

How to be Meritorious?

Excellence in studies and achieving Merit is a landmark of success in the lives of students. Student life is the only time when they can give a positive direction and shape up their career and personality. Hard work and dedication towards studies, goal setting and working towards it in a systematic manner is all that is required. Adopting, developing and implementing of good habits create self-confidence and courage and hence, it leads students towards success in every field.

Studying, Thinking and Evaluation

Thinking deeply, self-evaluation and solving of sample test papers on a regular basis is a must to understand the crux of the subject matter. Otherwise all the efforts and time devoted would get wasted and simply become a reading exercise only. Good learning will result into good retention which in-turn will help in good recalling of information during the exams. It will also result into faster speed in writing, finishing before stipulated time and revising thoroughly before handing over the answer sheets.

Coaching

Coaching is another systematic way of teaching and training students. It is quite different from the way normal teaching is carried out in the class. Good coaching comes at a hefty price. Studying pattern followed in the school is designed to take care of every student belonging to different socio-economic backgrounds, general aptitude and intellect. No student can be left out in the class. Therefore, students who wish to excel and be meritorious, approach coaching centres to further strengthen their knowledge and skills.

Coaching centres engage with themselves the best of intellectuals specialising in their specific fields and thus, form a team. They teach and train students through a variety

Today's Date: __ / __ / ____
(Kindly write with a Pencil)

of simple techniques and provide notes also. Considerable improvements have been noticed by the students themselves in their understanding as well as performance.

Solve Question Papers of Previous Years

Students should learn the art of understanding the format of question papers well before the exams, and the most suitable technique of answering the questions should be adopted. The best method is to solve the question papers of previous years repeatedly many times. Evaluate your own performance and take the guidance of your teachers to further improve your attempts, scoring and skills. It raises the confidence level of students to unimaginable heights. These question papers cover the whole syllabus and thus, also enable the revision several times.

Goal-Setting

One of the main ingredients of excellence in studies is goal setting and then extending the required efforts in a dedicated way. Goal-setting depends entirely on the student. The preparations required for studying will largely depend on the level of the goals to be achieved.

Some of the desires and goals could be staying ahead of others in the class since the very beginning. Also, concentrating on studies with optimum utilisation of resources available and not wandering here and there. It could also be scoring well in exams and being meritorious. Some others could wish for getting selected in the most renowned educational institution for higher studies whereas there could be some others who would like to be hired by the most sought after corporate group in the same country or abroad.

Utilisation of Time

Home and school are the only two places where students spend most of their time during the whole day. The time that is spent in school has been divided into various periods. The quality time that is available at home works out to be six hours approximately. This time has to be taken care of and utilised appropriately in studies to achieve maximum benefits. A time-table should be prepared at home also and followed strictly to maintain an edge in the class.

Similarly, all subjects should be studied with full alertness and concentration in the class. The absorption and grasping of knowledge is maximum in the classroom which should be taken benefit of. This is also proper utilisation of your time. This leads to recalling of things learnt in the class fast while answering the question paper.

Control Over Bad Habits and Emotions

Time and energy are the two important resources that are limited and always short in the life of students. It needs to be taken care of and hence, conserved and utilised properly.

There are some activities and emotions that should be controlled and neglected to avoid wastage of time. These also have adverse effects on your health. Some of these are indulging in sexual acts, anger, greed, jealousy, gambling or betting, intoxication and laziness or over-sleeping, etc. Students who wish to excel in their studies should maintain a comfortable distance from all such activities. They should also not befriend such people as well.

'A person is known by the company he keeps.'

Overcome Shortcomings and Mend Your Mistakes

Realising your own shortcomings and mistakes helps students to take appropriate and corrective measures in time. It also helps them a great deal during the final preparation days. Such steps will ensure good performance during the exams and hence, increase the chances of being meritorious.

Copying is Bad for Intellect

The concept of 'Knowledge is Power' fails badly where students develop the bad habit of copying and cheating. It proves to be a big deterrent in their learning as well. They also tend to lose their self-confidence and self-respect. And, ultimately these students will not be able to succeed much in life despite having scored well in their exams. Since, they are short on their knowledge they would find it difficult to prove their competency in their professional arena also.

Adopting of Good Habits

Adopting of good habits will lead students towards better opportunities, recognition, self-respect and success in their lives. These habits are:

1. Self-dependence and self-respect
2. Concentration in the class
3. Studying patiently and steadily
4. Always working happily
5. Stability in emotions
6. Early to bed and early to rise

7. Living and working as a team with other fellow students
8. Recognising and availing hidden opportunities in time
9. Hiding own secrets of success
10. Alertness towards studies
11. Alertness towards self-security and self-defence
12. Farsightedness
13. Courage
14. Remaining happy, contented and positive in all situations

Speed and Timing in Examinations

Knowledge without speed, and speed without knowledge, both are useless for students who wish to excel in studies and be meritorious in their exams. So, students should practise faster reading and writing during the regular course of their studies. In this way, they will develop good speed and practice committing lesser mistakes. In turn, it will help them to attempt all the questions correctly and stand a chance to be meritorious.

Small and easy questions should be attempted first so as to save and devote more time for difficult and lengthy questions. Time planning has to be done by the students themselves according to their abilities and the format of the question paper. A few minutes should always be spared for revision in the end. This ensures enough time for checking and elimination of mistakes or any leftover question.

Understand First, Then Attempt

Students should first read their question papers thoroughly and understand the questions. Then patiently re-number all the questions in the series they wish to answer. The time devoted in this activity will help in setting the timing of answering all the questions. This is the right method of attempting a question paper to score maximum marks.

Be Bold and Not Nervous

A very common thing noticed among some students just before the exams is getting nervous or even sick. This happens due to less confidence and certain other phobias developed in the mind of students towards their exams. But all this can be avoided very easily by just being attentive in the class during the year and thoroughly learning and revising the syllabus in small bits on a daily basis. This automatically increases self-confidence of students and they are now more than willing to face their exams.

Examination Promises Progress

Examination is a yardstick to evaluate the progress of studies and its learning by the students from time to time. Exams should be faced boldly and enthusiastically. This is the time when students come to know of their learning, their knowledge, their capabilities and finally, their competency. Exam time is also the time to cover up all that has been left behind in the syllabus. In a way it helps to complete the process of learning as well.

Attempting the Exams

It is the exams that are going to decide the future of children. So any carelessness can prove to be very harmful. Before attempting any competition or examination, the following steps should be taken into consideration:

- Final revision should be made to fine tune all that has been studied and prepared.
- Thoroughly check and mend one's tools and equipments a day before to avoid any delay or disruption later on. Some of these tools are writing board, pen, pencil, rubber, sharpener, scale, compass, geometry box, etc.
- It is advisable to keep one or two extra pen and pencils. And all the tools should be in proper working condition. It will save precious time and concentration at the time of writing the exam.
- Preferably, keep all these things one by one in a bag the previous night itself, so that nothing is left out at home when leaving for the exam in a state of hurry and nervousness.
- Also keep safely inside this bag your roll number and admission card required for entering the examination hall.
- Sleep early the night before the exam. It will help to avoid fatigue and burning sensation in the eyes, headache, excessive exam stress, etc. The students will also feel relaxed and refreshed during the exam which will help them to attempt all the questions with speed and alertness.
- Having light dinner at the night before the exam day could prove to be a boon. The food will get digested easily and quickly even when the mind is under pressure, and secondly it would ensure sound sleep.
- During exam days try to wake up a bit early and make a quick revision of all the notes. Enjoy your bath a little longer, meditate

for a few minutes and pray to God as per your beliefs and tradition. It does not waste or take up much time as it is believed to be by many.

- There are two main benefits provided by nature in doing so. Waking up and reading early in the morning keeps students refreshed throughout the day and the remembrance is far better. Secondly, during the bath, water cleanses and opens-up all the pores of the body, refreshes and energises the body, mind and soul. It enables alertness of their mind, faster retrieval of information and better speed in solving the question paper.
- Take a nourished but light breakfast before leaving for the exam. Breakfast is regarded as the most important fuel to start the day and it provides energy all day long.
- Students should also wear a watch which would prove beneficial in planning the timing of solving all the questions. It would always keep a check on the time left.
- Preferably, students should have the habit of using the wrist watch throughout the year. This will help them to train themselves in managing their time well.
- Students should leave their home quite early so as to reach the examination centre at least 15-30 minutes in advance. This will keep their anxiety under control, thus avoiding any kind of rush or extra pressure on the mind while travelling. The idea is to keep the body and the mind relaxed as much as possible.
- Students should enter the examination hall with great self-confidence. They should also make a commitment with themselves to be a topper and make it to the merit list. At this time they shouldn't feel or show any kind of nervousness.
- After finding the seat allocated to them students should make themselves comfortable. Now, take out all the permitted things required during the exam and handover the rest to the invigilator. .It is better to leave all the notes and study material at home itself so that it does not distract the students in any way when the exam has finally started.

All children who have the privilege of going to the school must remember that they have been provided with the most important tool which will shape-up their destiny and that is 'Education'.

In today's highly mechanised world it is impossible to walk even a single step forward if a person is not well educated and well mannered, leave aside being totally illiterate. Knowledge can be gained through formal education by attending the school regularly. The learned can do wonders for themselves as well as for the nation. Everyone has to follow the rules and regulations of the civilised society to live and earn in a dignified manner.

Advice: *Kindly read this chapter two to three times in order to understand the techniques suggested. You may even underline the important points for a quick reference later on.*

Easy Tips from the Author

Improving Your Memory is Very Simple and Easy.

-- Let us See How --

MEDITATION

↓

GOOD OBSERVATION

↓

GOOD LEARNING

↓

GOOD REMEMBERING

↓

GOOD RECALLING

↓

GOOD PERFORMANCE

↓

GOOD MARKS – GOOD GRADES

BEING MERITORIOUS

↓

SUCCESS * RECOGNITION * RESPECT

CONFIDENCE * HAPPINESS

Great Memory Tip for Life:

Soak 5-7 almonds in water every night. Peel them in the morning and eat every day. And See the Magic.

The following exercises can be undertaken and practised by everyone. But it will make more sense and be more useful to those who have gone through the whole book. Because the idea and logic would be clear only after going through all the chapters one by one on a daily basis. This is not an ordinary book, but a complete Memory Improvement Program compiled for your convenience in an easy, readable format.

For example, whenever we repeatedly see some of the interesting clips from famous movies, they generally do not create much fun. But when we come across the same while watching whole of the movie then such clips entertain us more. Hence, kindly read this book slowly and follow the instructions carefully to benefit from it in the true sense.

Following are the activities which can be practised daily for further improving your memory power. This is in addition to the *30-Day Memory Improvement Program* which should be repeated at least 4-6 times at an interval of 1-2 months only.

People are generally aware of the physical exercises only. Hence, the following exercises will open up your way of thinking and importance about the exercises for the mind as well. Some of the exercises and methods will gradually become an important part of your daily life. Then, we can think and feel that this book has served its purpose for you in its true sense.

Indulge Your Mind in Some Guesswork (with your eyes closed)

- Often try to recognise local currency coins in your pocket.
- Often try to distinguish between the different vehicles passing by.
- Often try to recognise various flowers as per their fragrances in a park.
- Often try to guess the change in temperatures at home and other places.
- Often try to recall all the routine activities while bathing.
- Often try to guess what all has been served to you during your meals.
- Often try to guess and ascertain the timings during the day.

Try Using the Other Hand

- Try to play games and sports with the other hand.
- Try eating your meals, writing, drawing or painting with a brush, playing a musical instrument, etc. with your other hand.

- Try to switch on your TV and other devices, etc. with the other hand. Also try using remote control devices with the other hand.
- Try combing your hair, shaving, brushing your teeth, brushing your shoes, dialling a number, etc. with your other hand.
- Try cutting, peeling or eating fruits and vegetables, etc. with your other hand.

General Activities

- Solve different kinds of puzzles.
- Participate in group plays, acting, song and dance competitions, debates and lectures, etc.
- Participate in science exhibitions, competitions, seminars, fairs, matches, fetes, games and sports.
- Start a new hobby.
- Observe plants, flowers, insects, birds and animals, etc.
- Imitate an actor, a celebrity or a famous personality.
- Try dribbling the basket ball or any other ball in a new way.
- Solve crossword puzzles or play scrabble where various combinations of words have to be formed.
- Start reading detective stories and novels. Also start watching detective serials and movies.
- Collect information about the inventions and discoveries currently taking place.
- Maintain a record of your daily expenses.
- Start counting the stairs in your subconscious mind wherever you go.
- At what time you woke up in the morning? = ...

  What all you had in your breakfast? = ...

  Are you feeling comfortable in your dress? = Yes/ No/Okay

  What you liked about yourself today? = ...
- Try noting down and memorising the alpha-numeric registration number of the vehicles parked nearby your house. Gradually, find out which vehicle belongs to your immediate neighbours and the rest to others.
- Start noting down in your mind all the things present in the room

when you visit some public office, exhibition, museums, fairs, fetes, hotels and restaurants, etc. Afterwards note it down on a paper or your diary.

- How many steps are there in the stairs of your building and your school.
- What is the normal time taken to reach the nearest bus stop, park or supermarket if you go walking, by your bicycle or by your car.
- How much time do you generally take to get ready when you are going to your school or office, to play, to the market or when going to attend some party or a function.
- Generally what is your heart beat or pulse rate when you have just woken up, back from school or office, after outdoor sports or exercising, after cooking or gardening, before and after meals, after prayers or meditation, etc.
- Read the intended topic at a greater speed. This will be done as a practice to increase your speed.
- Gradually, the mind will get trained to read and understand the subjects faster. Hence, the need for repeating the same text afterwards will soon diminish and finish.
- Always remain active and alert in your activities. Gradually you will start feeling a gush of self-confidence increasing inside you.

Methods to Improve Your Decisions

- Start keeping a small pocket diary.
- Note down the pending works.
- Always seek and hire the advice and services of a professional.
- Try to analyse and solve problems with a different perspective.
- Never take decisions in haste or due to shortage of time.
- Never take decisions when you are being pressurised by others.
- Never take decisions in a state of intoxication or while feeling tired or worried.

Methods to Improve Your Concentration

- Undertake only one activity at a time whenever possible.
- Always wear neat and clean clothes to feel comfortable.
- Always take lighter meals preferably 4-5 times during the day

instead of the regular 2 or 3 heavy meals.

- Try to avoid too much oily, spicy, cold or fast food.
- Prefer home cooked food for most of the time. Also, eat food when it is being served hot.
- Use natural light for most of the time.
- Never compromise on your sleeping hours.
- Adopt and follow a simple and positive attitude towards life.
- Try to choose the right time and atmosphere to start up any new assignment.

Avoid Forgetting

- Be cautious and alert in your approach towards your preparations.
- Do not over exert yourself or put extra load on your mind.
- Take frequent breaks in between studying.
- Try keeping your haircut as short as possible.

Do's:

- Study with your room closed.
- A quick short bath energises the body and mind simultaneously.
- Subjects, topics or chapters should be interchanged at regular intervals.
- Undertake light Physical exercises for 10-15 minutes only.
- A nap for 10-15 minutes.
- Take lighter meals.

Don'ts:

- Refreshment breaks should not exceed more than five minutes at the most.
- Never ever think of consuming tobacco of any kind, cigarette smoking or alcohol, drugs, etc.
- Even drinking tea, coffee or cold drinks should be limited.
- The direction of the light should not enter and disturb your eyes directly.

Keep Worries and Tensions Away

- Confide your worries in someone trustworthy

- Do not sit idle or remain alone for longer durations
- Holidaying
- Undertake one task at a time
- Neglect unimportant issues and gossips
- Do not interfere in others' affairs
- Talk less and listen more
- Face problems with peace and patience
- Do not be narrow-minded
- Always use a table lamp
- Always use an alarm clock

-- Final Advice --

Always Say to Yourself
Till It Becomes Your Habit

* * * * *

YES, I CAN DO IT
&
YES, I WILL DO IT

***

The Best of Self Help Books

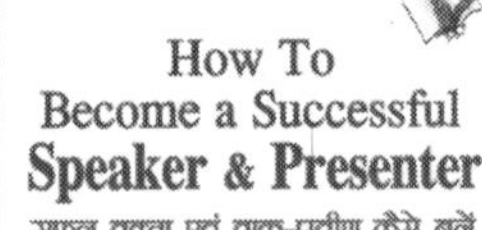

How to Become a Successful Speaker & Presenter

Format: Paperback
Language: English
Pages: 112

The book ***How to become a Successful Speaker & Presenter*** has carefully dissected every aspect of public speaking and presents a clear map that any aspiring speaker can follow.

You will master 'How to'

- Conquer stage fright
- Organize material in a flowing manner
- Customise speech for different sets of gathering
- Inspire audience
- Include humour and maintain eye contact
- Involve people interactively
- Maintain friendly yet professional image, tone and diction
- Invite queries

How to become a Successful Speaker & Presenter has been carefully thought out to make an easy and interesting read to leave you buzzing with ideas on how you can implement the ideas and plans for speaking effectively in public.

The Complete Guide To Group Discussion

Author: Prof. Shrikant Prasoon
Format: Paperback
Language: English
Pages: 200

Group Discussions (GD) are commonly used to assess several personality aspects of candidates during various entrance tests and as a part of selection process for various jobs. This comprehensive guide book helps you clear the fog surrounding GD and its step-by-step instructions will make you a winner in GD.

- Insight into: Need of GD, Do's & Don'ts in GD, Body Language & Public Speaking, Skills & Ability required in GD, and so on
- Important GD topics, How to gather Information for GD, Reading & Practice for GD
- Practical tips on GD Preparation & Participation

Go Ahead, Enjoy Reading and Be a Winner!!!

www.vspublishers.com